KS3
French

Complete Revision
and Practice

Contents

Contents

Published by CGP

Editors:
Rachel Selway, Jennifer Underwood

Contributors:
Chris Dennett, Sarah Donachie, Simon Little, Bettina Hermoso-Gomez, Becky May, Claire Thompson, Nadia Waller, Gillian Wallis, James Paul Wallis and Chrissy Williams.

With thanks to Latefa Mansarit, Sam Norman and Helen Smith for the proofreading.

Audio CD recorded, edited and mastered at Bright Blue Studios by Charley Darbishire, featuring the voices of Floriane Blot, Pierre-Emmanuel Leng, Leanore De Maleprade, Remi Nouailles.

ISBN: 978 1 84146 436 7

Groovy website: www.cgpbooks.co.uk
Jolly bits of clipart from CorelDRAW®
Printed by Elanders Ltd, Newcastle upon Tyne

Based on the classic CGP style created by Richard Parsons.

Numbers

Welcome to page 1. It's got some really useful stuff on it, so here goes:

Learn the numbers — **les nombres**

1	un		11	onze
2	deux		12	douze
3	trois		13	treize
4	quatre		14	quatorze
5	cinq		15	quinze
6	six		16	seize
7	sept		17	dix-sept
8	huit		18	dix-huit
9	neuf		19	dix-neuf
10	dix		20	vingt

The French words for 11-16 all end 'ze'. The words for 17-19 all mean 'ten-seven' etc.

20	vingt			
30	trente			
40	quarante			
50	cinquante		21	vingt-et-un
60	soixante		22	vingt-deux
70	soixante-dix		23	vingt-trois
80	quatre-vingts		24	vingt-quatre
90	quatre-vingt-dix		25	vingt-cinq
100	cent			

Most 'ten-type' numbers end in 'nte' (except vingt). 70-90 are weird — 70 is 'sixty-ten', 80 is 'four twenties' and 90 is 'four-twenty-ten'.

The 'in-between' numbers are like in English — just remember 'et-un' for numbers ending in 1.

70	soixante-dix		90	quatre-vingt-dix
71	soixante et onze		91	quatre-vingt-onze
72	soixante-douze		92	quatre-vingt-douze
73	soixante-treize			

For the 70s and 90s, you need the teens — 70 is '60-ten', and 71 is '60 and eleven'.

This is one of the most important things to learn

That's why we've put it on page 1. If you're not sure of your numbers, you're going to have problems with telling the time, shopping, phone numbers, directions... lots of things, actually.

Numbers

You need to be able to say things like 'first floor', 'second on the left'...

1st — premier or première

Saying 'first' is a bit tricky to learn. You use 'premier' to talk about a masculine thing, and 'première' to talk about a feminine thing.

premier   = first (masculine)

première   = first (feminine)

Add -ième to a number for second, third etc.

Luckily, there's a simple rule for saying 'second', 'third' and so on:

NUMBER + 'ième'

deuxième   = second

troisième   = third

For example:

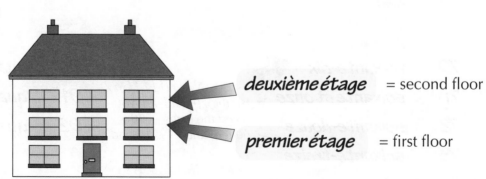

deuxième étage   = second floor

premier étage   = first floor

Just think of the 'premier' league to remember this one
See — it's amazing how many French words we've stolen to use in English. You'll spot loads as you go through this book. They are often pronounced differently though, so watch out.

Time

Now that you've got the hang of numbers, you can learn to <u>tell the time</u> in French.

Learn all the clock times

Telling the time in French is dull but <u>necessary</u>.

The French don't say am and pm — they use the 24-hour clock instead. So 4am would be 'quatre heures' and 4pm would be 'seize heures'.

deux heures = two o'clock

One o'clock is the odd one out. There's no 's' on the heures bit.

une heure = one o'clock

Say the o'clock bit, then stick these on the end.

deux heures et demie = half past two

quarter past: ...et quart
ten past: ...dix

Talking about <u>minutes to</u> is a bit more tricky. You're basically saying 2 o'clock minus (moins) a quarter, two o'clock minus 10 minutes, and so on.

deux heures moins le quart = quarter to two

ten to: ...moins dix

What time is it? — **Quelle heure est-il?**

Quelle heure est-il? = What time is it?

Il est deux heures. = It's two o'clock.

Times are another thing teachers love to ask you about
Honestly, you'd think that no one had a watch of their own, the way you're expected to answer 'Quelle heure est-il?' all the time. 'Achetez une montre' is the best reply, I reckon.

Times and Dates

Other times

hier = yesterday

aujourd'hui = today

le jour = day

demain = tomorrow

la semaine = week

le matin = morning

le mois = month

l'année = year

l'après-midi = afternoon

le soir = evening

la nuit = night

Days of the week

There are <u>no capital letters</u> for the days of the week in French:

lundi	*mardi*	*mercredi*	*jeudi*	*vendredi*
Monday	Tuesday	Wednesday	Thursday	Friday

samedi	*dimanche*
Saturday	Sunday

To say '<u>on Mondays</u>' you put 'le' and the day:

Je joue le lundi = I play on Mondays

To say '<u>on Monday</u>' you just put the day:

Jouons lundi = Let's play on Monday

Now you can invite a French kid on a date

It stands to reason really, but you're never going to get away without knowing the days of the week in French. There are only seven of them, after all, so you haven't got any excuses.

Times and Dates

You can learn the months of the year in groups of four. They're <u>similar</u> (ish) to the English, which helps.

Months of the year

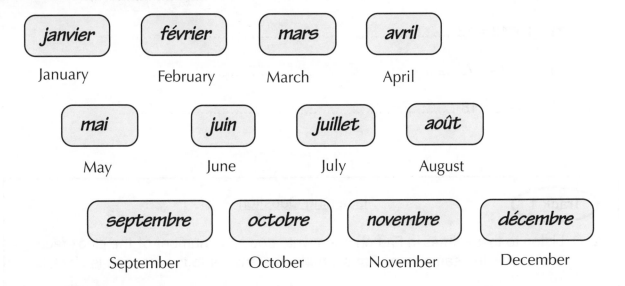

janvier	**février**	**mars**	**avril**
January	February	March	April
mai	**juin**	**juillet**	**août**
May	June	July	August
septembre	**octobre**	**novembre**	**décembre**
September	October	November	December

Dates

Dates come up all the time. For example <u>booking holidays</u> (p.101) and your <u>birthday</u> (p.17). There are a couple of things to learn.

1)   You don't say 'the third of May', you say 'the three May'.

le trois mai   = the third of May   **le douze août**   = the twelfth of August

2)   The first of the month is a bit different.
You do say 'the first May' or 'the first August'.

le premier mai   = the first of May

And now dates — this stuff is never-ending
I suppose it all comes in handy for reminding French people when your birthday is, so that they can buy you lots of presents and a big cake. It's pretty basic stuff, but it comes in really handy.

6

Practice Questions

1   Write out these sums in words, in French. The first one has been done for you.

a)   2 + 3 = 5   *deux + trois = cinq* ....

b)   4 + 7 = 11 ....

c)   1 + 12 = 13 ....

d)   9 + 8 = 17 ....

e)   20 - 2 = 18 ....

Track 1

Listening Question

2   Listen to these times in French, then write down the number of the clock face that shows the same time. For example, the answer to the first one is clock 3.

1

2

3

4

5

6

---

3   Write out these dates in French:

a)   3rd August

b)   10th April

c)   25th December

d)   14th March

e)   18th February

f)   31st October

g)   1st July

h)   27th January

Meeting and Greeting

You probably think that you know how to say <u>hello</u> in French already.
But there's a bit <u>more</u> to it than a simple '<u>bonjour</u>':

Saying Hello — **Bonjour**

Saying hello starts off most conversations — brush up your
<u>social skills</u> and learn the different ways of saying it.

bonjour　= hello

This is quite a <u>formal</u> way of saying 'hello'. It literally means 'good day'.

salut　= hi

This is <u>less formal</u>. It's the sort of thing you'd say to your <u>mates</u>.

There are different 'hellos' for different times of the day

bonjour　= good morning / good day

bonsoir　= good evening

bonne nuit　= good night

You can use all these 'hello' words either on their own, or with a <u>name</u>.
E.g. bonjour Madame / bonsoir Nicole / salut Pierre etc.

Don't just say 'bonjour' all the time — it's dull

Bonjour is OK, but every Tom, Dick or Harry uses it, so mix it up a bit and sound a bit cooler by
saying stuff like 'salut' when you meet someone your own age. It sounds much more natural.

Meeting and Greeting

Now you get to learn to say <u>goodbye</u>. Great — now you can get shot of your penpal.

Saying Goodbye — **Au Revoir**

If you've said hello, you need to be able to say <u>goodbye</u> too.
Some phrases are more <u>formal</u> than others:

This is quite <u>formal</u> — it literally means 'until we meet again'.

au revoir = goodbye

Both of these are more <u>casual</u>.

à bientôt = see you soon

à plus tard = see you later

How are you? — **Comment ça va?**

These phrases all mean '<u>How are you?</u>':

Comment vas-tu? = This is how the French say 'How are you?' Literally it means '<u>how are you going?</u>' Only use it with someone <u>younger</u> than or the <u>same age</u> as you.

Comment allez-vous? = Same as the one above, but for when you're speaking to <u>more than one person</u> or to someone <u>older</u> than you.

Comment ça va? = This is a bit less formal. It literally means '<u>How's it going?</u>'

Ça va? = This is a <u>shortened</u> version.

You've got loads of choice here

It looks like even saying 'how are you?' is a lot more complicated than you might think.
Don't panic — none of these are hard to say, it's just a question of picking the right one.

Meeting and Greeting

Time for a bit more <u>small talk</u>. 'May I present my friend Billy. Ooh, pleased to meet you.'
Blah blah blah. You get the picture.

Introducing People — **Je vous présente...**

Sometimes you might have to <u>introduce someone</u>. Here's how:

Je vous présente Isabelle.   = Let me introduce Isabelle.

Je vous présente mon ami. Il s'appelle Jacques.

= Let me introduce my friend. He's called Jacques.

If you're speaking to someone your age or younger you would say, 'Je te présente...'
(But it would still be 'vous' if there's more than one person your age.)

Pleased to meet you — **Enchanté(e)**

When you're introduced to someone, reply with '<u>pleased to meet you</u>'
and sound really <u>impressive</u>.

Enchanté(e)   = Pleased to meet you.

You write that second 'e' on the end if you're a girl.
It sounds the same when you say it though.

It pays to be polite
Well, OK it probably doesn't pay, as such, but it's definitely a good idea. If you go to France
you'll meet a bunch of new people, and you'll have to say all the right things to them.

Being Polite

Don't forget your Ps and Qs

Make sure you're <u>polite</u> by using the words for <u>please</u> and <u>thank you</u>.

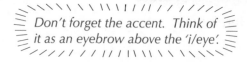

Don't forget the accent. Think of it as an eyebrow above the 'i/eye'.

s'il vous plaît   = please (formal or to more than one person)

s'il te plaît   = please (informal)

Louise, je voudrais du fromage, s'il vous plaît.

= I'd like some cheese please Louise.

Deux billets, s'il vous plaît.

= Two tickets please.

Always say thank you

You'll probably want to <u>thank</u> people when you're in France. Here's how:

Merci (beaucoup)   = thank you (very much)

You won't get far without 'please' and 'thank you'
The French are pretty polite, so you need to use these words quite a bit. Just remember to say 's'il vous plaît' whenever you ask for things, and 'merci' when you get them. Easy.

Being Polite

Don't mention it — De rien

A really <u>easy</u> way to sound polite is to learn this simple phrase. When someone thanks you, reply with:

> **De rien.** = Don't mention it / it was nothing.

Saying sorry — Je suis désolé(e)

Chances are you'll have to <u>apologise</u> for something at some point. Effective <u>grovelling</u> is a very handy skill in any language. Learn these <u>two different ways</u> of saying you're sorry:

> **Je suis désolé(e).** = I'm sorry.

> **Je suis désolé(e), mais j'ai oublié votre nom.**
>> = I'm sorry, but I've forgotten your name.

> **Excusez-moi.** = I'm sorry.

> **Excusez-moi mais je n'aime pas les fraises.**
>> = I'm sorry, but I don't like strawberries.

> 'Excusez-moi' can also mean 'excuse me', if you're wanting to get someone's attention.
> E.g. 'Excusez-moi, monsieur, où est la banque, s'il vous plaît?'
>> = Excuse me, Sir, where is the bank, please?
>
> You can also use '<u>pardon</u>' instead of 'excusez-moi'.
> E.g. 'Pardon, madame, quelle heure est-il?'.
>> = Excuse me, Madam, what time is it?

It can be hard to work out which phrase to use
Sometimes it's a bit difficult to work out exactly which way to say sorry in French. If you bump into someone in the street, they'll probably say 'pardon' and never ever 'je suis désolé'.

Being Polite

If you want to be <u>polite</u>, you need to know how to ask for things in a <u>nice way</u>:

I would like — Je voudrais

It's loads better to say '<u>I would like</u>' (je voudrais) than '<u>I want</u>' (je veux).

Je voudrais du pain.   = I would like some bread.

You can also say that you'd like to do something:

Je voudrais + INFINITIVE

Je voudrais <u>jouer</u> au tennis.   = I would like <u>to play</u> tennis.

Je voudrais <u>parler</u>.   = I would like <u>to talk</u>.

Je voudrais <u>aller</u> au cinéma.   = I would like <u>to go</u> to the cinema.

Je voudrais manger du chocolat
Yes, 'je voudrais' is the best, and politest, way to get exactly what you want when you're in France. It'll also score you loads of marks in class, so get that phrase learnt right now.

Being Polite

May I? — Est-ce que je peux...?

A good way of sounding polite is by asking <u>permission</u> to do things.
There's a special rule for saying 'May I...?'.

Est-ce que je peux + INFINITIVE

Est-ce que je peux manger du chocolat, s'il vous plaît?

= May I eat some chocolate, please?

Est-ce que je peux regarder la télévision, s'il vous plaît?

= May I watch TV, please?

Learn how to be polite when you're a guest

You need to know how to be a <u>model guest</u> in France. Asking if you can <u>help</u> with anything is a good start:

Est-ce que je peux vous aider à *faire la cuisine ?* = Can I help you with the cooking?

> *do the washing-up:* faire la vaisselle
> *lay the table:* mettre la table

If you really need to <u>complain</u> about something, make sure you do it politely —
be <u>apologetic</u> (see p. 11):

Excusez-moi, mais je suis végétarien(ne) / je ne mange pas de viande.

= I'm sorry, but I'm vegetarian / I don't eat meat.

Excusez-moi, mais je ne parle pas français
That means 'I'm sorry, but I don't speak French', in case you didn't work it out. So that's not a phrase you'll be needing once you've worked your way through this book. Hurrah.

Practice Questions

1 Write down the best words to say in these situations.
Choose from the words in the box.

   a) You meet your best friend in the morning.

   b) You speak to your parents before going to bed.

   c) You say goodbye to a stranger you met on a bus.

   d) You meet your school teacher on the way to school.

   e) You say goodbye to your friend who you are going to see soon.

| salut | au revoir | bonjour | à bientôt | bonne nuit |

2 Write these sentences in French.

   a) Hi Gérard, how's it going?

   b) Good evening, pleased to meet you.

   c) Let me introduce my friend.

   d) See you later.

   e) He's called Robert.

   f) Good night, my friends.

   g) Let me introduce Henri.

 Track 2   Listening Question

3 Listen to these five conversations, then for each one write down if the statement
is true (T) or false (F):

   a) Sophie and Monsieur Dupont are talking in the morning.

   b) Emilie and Marc are saying goodbye to each other.

   c) Madame Ferret has met André before.

   d) Robert and Gaëlle know each other quite well.

   e) This is an informal conversation.

15

15

Practice Questions

4 Copy out the words in the boxes, then draw lines to join together the two halves of each sentence. The first one has been done for you.

Merci	quelle heure est-il?
Je voudrais	je n'aime pas les fraises.
Excusez-moi, mais	s'il vous plaît.
Deux cafés	beaucoup.
Pardon, monsieur,	du beurre.

Track 3   <u>Listening Question</u>

5 Listen to these four apologies, then write down the number of the picture that matches each apology. The first one has been done for you.

a) [2]   b) [ ]   c) [ ]   d) [ ]

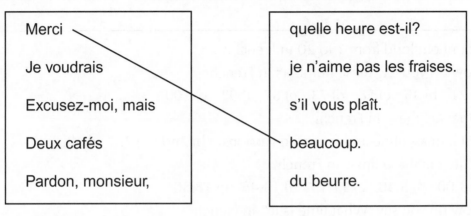

1   2   3   4

6 Write these sentences in French, using 'May I' — 'Est-ce que je peux...'.

a) May I go to the cinema?

b) May I do the washing-up?

c) May I do the cooking?

d) May I lay the table?

Summary Questions

Thought you'd finished the section? Think again, it's time to <u>test</u> what's lodged in your brain and what's fallen straight out. This section covers all the basic bits and bobs that you need. If you don't get this stuff sorted, everything else will be harder.

1) Count out loud from 1 to 20 in French.

2) How do you say these numbers in French?

a) 21   b) 35   c) 58   d) 73   e) 87   f) 92   g) 100

3) What are these in French?

a) 1st (masculine and feminine versions)   b) 2nd   c) 3rd   d) 4th

4) Write out these times in French.

a) 3:00   b) 5:30   c) 11:15   d) 13:45   e) 18:50

5) How do you say 'What time is it?' in French?

6) What are these in French?

a) today   b) tomorrow   c) yesterday   d) morning   e) afternoon

7) Write out the days of the week in French from Monday to Sunday.

8) Translate into French:

a) I play on Tuesdays   b) I'm playing on Saturday.

9) Write out the months of the year in French, from January to December.

10) Write in French:

a) today's date   b) the date of your birthday.

11) What do these words mean in English?

a) bonjour   b) salut   c) bonsoir

12) Give three different ways of saying goodbye in French and say if they are formal or casual.

13) Write out four ways of saying 'How are you?' in French.
Which ones would you use if you were speaking to more than one person?

14) How would you introduce your friend to:

a) someone your age   b) someone older than you?

15) What is the French word that means 'pleased to meet you' (masculine and feminine versions)?

16) What are these in French?

a) please   b) thank you   c) don't mention it

17) Write a sentence which includes the French word for 'please' in it.

18) Give two French phrases each for:

a) I'm sorry   b) excuse me.

19) How would you say that you wanted some tomatoes in a polite way?

20) In French, ask permission to:

a) play football   b) listen to the radio   c) go shopping

21) How would you offer to help your host to do:

a) the cooking   b) the washing up?

Your Details

Most of this section is talking about yourself. All you bigheads, this one's for you...

Talking about yourself — facts and figures

You have to be able to answer these questions all about <u>yourself</u>.
The bits in <u>green</u> are the bits you'll need to <u>change</u> (unless you <u>are</u> Bruce).

Comment tu t'appelles?   = What are you called?

Je m'appelle Bruce .   = I'm called Bruce.

Quel âge as-tu?   = How old are you?

J'ai quatorze ans.   = I'm fourteen.

Quelle est la date de ton anniversaire?   = When is your birthday?

Mon anniversaire est le trois mai .   = My birthday is the 3rd of May.

For more numbers
and dates, see
pages 1-5.

Qu'est-ce que tu aimes?   = What do you like?

J'aime la musique .   = I like music.

You can bung anything in here, like sports
(p.72), hobbies (p.74) or foods (p.56-59).

Make sure you learn these phrases — they're vitally important

You'd better remember these questions, and their answers. You're going to see them a lot in
the future. I guarantee you'll get asked at least one in your oral exam if you take GCSE French.

Describe Yourself

And now you get to tell everyone how wonderful and beautiful you are...

Say what you **look like**

You need to be able to describe things like your <u>size</u>, <u>eyes</u> and <u>hair</u>. Come on, be honest.

Je suis **grand(e)** *.* = I am tall.

tall: grand(e)	*fat:* gros(se)
small: petit(e)	*thin:* mince
medium height: de taille moyenne	

<u>Add</u> the bits in brackets if you're <u>female</u> (see p.126).

J'ai les yeux **bleus** *.* = I have blue eyes.

blue: bleus   *green:* verts   *brown:* marron

J'ai les cheveux **noirs** *.* = I have black hair.

black: noirs	*short:* courts
red: roux	*shoulder-length:* mi-longs
blonde: blonds	*quite long:* assez longs

Je porte des lunettes. = I wear glasses.

Je ne porte pas de lunettes. = I don't wear glasses.

Describe your **personality**

Je suis...

= I am...

shy:	timide
nice:	sympa
hard-working:	travailleur / travailleuse
lazy:	paresseux / paresseuse
sporty:	sportif / sportive

Use these if you're <u>male</u>.   Use these if you're <u>female</u>.

Your Family

It can't all be about you — you have to talk about other people a bit too. Like your family.

Use these words for your **friends** and **family**

You can choose your <u>friends</u>, but you can't choose your <u>family</u>... Or something.

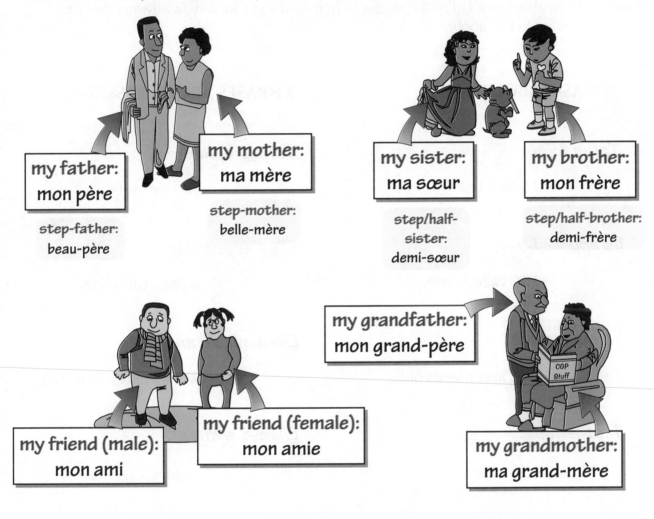

my father:
mon père

step-father:
beau-père

my mother:
ma mère

step-mother:
belle-mère

my sister:
ma sœur

step/half-sister:
demi-sœur

my brother:
mon frère

step/half-brother:
demi-frère

my friend (male):
mon ami

my friend (female):
mon amie

my grandfather:
mon grand-père

my grandmother:
ma grand-mère

CGP Stuff

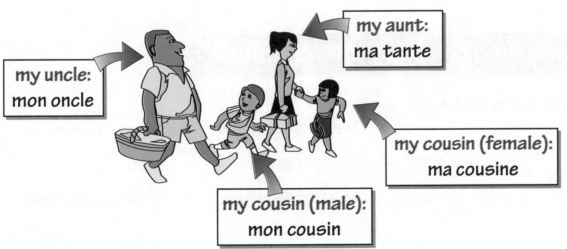

my uncle:
mon oncle

my aunt:
ma tante

my cousin (female):
ma cousine

my cousin (male):
mon cousin

This stuff's easy — nothing to worry about
You'd expect 'my female friend' to be 'ma amie', but that's <u>too hard to say</u>. It's like how you say 'an orange' in English, not 'a orange'. See p.129 for more on mon / ma / mes.

Your Family

Here's how to talk about your family and friends. If you really want to.

Say what your **family** and **friends** are like

I've written these phrases out <u>twice</u> so you can see the bits that <u>change</u> depending <u>who</u> you're talking about — a <u>lad</u> or a <u>lass</u>. Swap <u>frère</u> and <u>sœur</u> for any family member or friend you want to talk about.

PHRASES ABOUT LADS

J'ai un frère.

= I have a brother.

Il s'appelle Dave.

= He's called Dave.

Il a quinze ans.

= He's fifteen years old.

Il est sympa.

= He's nice.

PHRASES ABOUT LASSES

J'ai une sœur.

= I have a sister.

Elle s'appelle Liz.

= She's called Liz.

Elle a quinze ans.

= She's fifteen years old.

Elle est sympa.

= She's nice.

Only children get to say they're **unique**

If you're an <u>only child</u>, say:

Je suis fils unique. = I'm an only child (male).

OR

Je suis fille unique. = I'm an only child (female).

Only children have less to learn here — and no brother problems
You'll get bored of describing your brothers and sisters as 'kind' and 'nice' after a while.
Why not look up some more appropriate words? 'Ugly', 'smelly' and 'horrible' spring to mind.

Pets and Animals

This is better. You get to talk about cute animals. Useful for talking about your pets, and if someone tries to serve you "tortue" for dinner, you'll know they're up to no good.

Learn the pets — **Les animaux domestiques**

You should know the names of all these animals.

dog:
le chien

rabbit:
le lapin

tortoise:
la tortue

cat:
le chat

mouse:
la souris

horse:
le cheval

bird:
l'oiseau*

*=le+oiseau

hamster:
le hamster

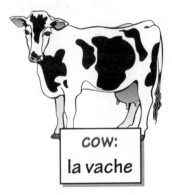

cow:
la vache

Luckily you can do without the French for porcupine, or alligator
If you don't have any pets, you could just pretend you do. Or if your pet isn't here (e.g. if you've got a pet hippo), pick an easy one instead, or look yours up in a dictionary and learn it.

Pets and Animals

And now you get to learn how to tell people about your pets. How very civilised.

I have a dog — J'ai un chien

You need to <u>understand</u> people talking about their <u>pets</u>, and talk about <u>yours</u> if you have one. I've used "chien" as an example — swap in the animal word for the pet you want to talk about.

1)   *J'ai un chien.*   = I have a dog.

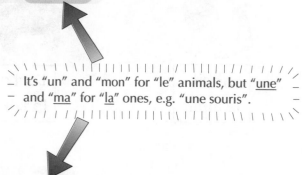

It's "un" and "mon" for "le" animals, but "<u>une</u>" and "<u>ma</u>" for "<u>la</u>" ones, e.g. "une souris".

2)   *Mon chien s'appelle 'Fido'.*   = My dog is called 'Fido'.

3)   *Je n'ai pas d'animaux domestiques.*   = I don't have a pet.

4)   *Mon chien est petit.*   = My dog is small.

sweet:	mignon(ne)
nasty:	méchant(e)
big:	grand(e)
black:	noir(e)

Learn all these animals, then give yourself a pet on the back

It's quite likely that your pet is something other than sweet, nasty, big, small or black. So you should learn some other colours (p. 67) and some other describing words (p.112).

Your Home

Now it's time to learn the French words for the different parts of the house — vital if you ever find yourself playing Cluedo in France.

Talk about the rooms in your house — **les pièces**

These are the 6 rooms you need to learn.
Well OK, 5 rooms if you're going to be picky...

['la pièce' = room]

kitchen:
la cuisine

bedroom:
la chambre

bathroom:
la salle de bains

dining room:
la salle à manger

living room:
le salon

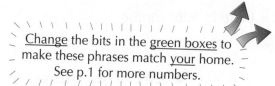

garden:
le jardin

In my home — **Chez moi**

Use '<u>chez moi</u>' to say 'my home' and '<u>chez toi</u>' for 'your home'.

Remember — it's <u>un</u> for 'le' words, and <u>une</u> for 'la' words.

Qu'est-ce qu'il y a chez toi?   = What is there in your home?

Chez moi, il y a une cuisine, un salon et deux chambres.

= In my home, there is a kitchen, a living room and two bedrooms.

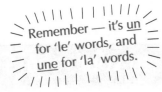

Change the bits in the green boxes to make these phrases match <u>your</u> home. See p.1 for more numbers.

Chez moi, il y a cinq pièces.

= In my home, there are five rooms.

Chez moi, il y a une souris dans la cuisine

There are <u>plurals</u> (see p.116) lurking in those example sentences. For the words here, the plurals are easy — just add an '<u>s</u>'. If you've got two <u>bathrooms</u>, that's 'deux salle<u>s</u> de bains'.

The Furniture

Now for a really thrilling subject. Furniture. Great. Just think about all those parties you might go to where you can impress people with your furniture anecdotes...

Talk about the furniture — les meubles

'Meubles' is a silly word, isn't it. Anyway, here are 'les meubles' you need to learn:

table:
la table

chair:
la chaise

bed:
le lit

sofa:
le canapé

cupboard:
le placard

wardrobe:
l'armoire (f.)

In your room — Dans ta chambre

Learn this <u>question</u>, and how to <u>answer</u> it. <u>Change</u> the <u>green box</u> to make it match <u>your</u> room — choose from the furniture above.
...And remember — <u>un</u> for 'le' words, and <u>une</u> for 'la' words.

Qu'est-ce qu'il y a dans ta chambre? = What is there in your room?

Il y a une table, un lit et deux chaises. = There is a table, a bed and two chairs.

Talk about the furniture — you'll be the life and soul of the party
You'd be surprised how little you'll need to talk about furniture in real conversations with real French people. But never mind, it is quite nice to know the French for 'wardrobe', just in case.

Practice Questions

1 Write down in English what each of these people are saying about themselves.

a)  Je suis sportive. J'aime le football.

b)  Je suis timide mais sympa.

c)  Je suis paresseuse. J'aime la musique.

d)  Je suis travailleur. J'aime l'école.

2 Write a sentence in French to answer each of these questions about yourself.

a) Comment tu t'appelles?

b) Quel âge as-tu?

c) Quelle est la date de ton anniversaire?

3 Write sentences in French describing yourself as if you were each of these people.

a) Daphne — tall, green eyes, red hair.

b) Velma — small, fat, brown eyes, wears glasses.

c) Fred — medium height, thin, blue eyes and blonde hair.

d) Mr. Shaggy — tall, quite long hair, green eyes.

Track 4

Listening Question

4 Listen to Marc talking about his family.

Then write down the names of his family members a) - f) to fill in the gaps in the family tree. Choose from the names in the box.

Jean-Luc
Michel
Chantal
Marie
Julien
Emilie

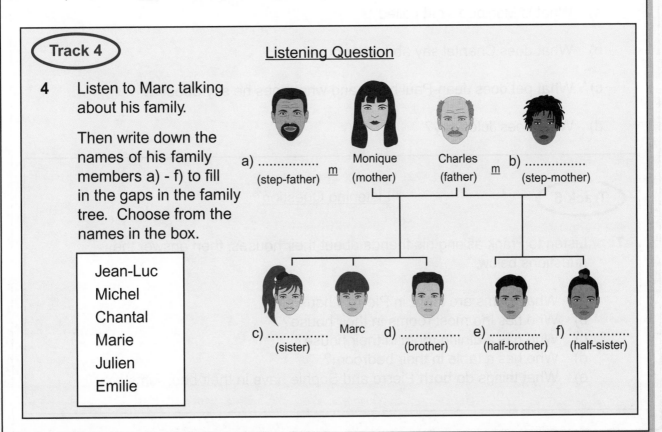

a) .... (step-father) — m — Monique (mother)   Charles (father) — m — b) .... (step-mother)

c) .... (sister)   Marc   d) .... (brother)   e) .... (half-brother)   f) .... (half-sister)

Practice Questions

5 Here are some adverts for lost pets. Imagine you're their owner and write sentences in French to describe each one. (The first one has been done for you.)

a)

> A big, black dog called Fang. If found take care – he can get nasty!

a) *J'ai un chien. Mon chien s'appelle Fang. Il est grand, noir et méchant.*

b)

> A small, green tortoise, called Fred.

c)

> A hamster, small, sweet, called Bubbles.

d)

> A bird, called Nipper, very nasty.

6 Read what these people say about their pets, then answer the questions below.

Jules — Je n'ai pas d'animaux domestiques.

Jean-Paul — J'ai une souris. Ma souris est mignonne.

Monique — J'ai un chat. Mon chat s'appelle 'Tom'.

Chantal — J'ai un chien. Mon chien est grand et méchant.

a) What is Monique's cat called?

b) What does Chantal say about her dog?

c) What pet does Jean-Paul have, and what does he say about it?

d) What does Jules say?

Track 5   <u>Listening Question</u>

7 Listen to Frank asking his friends about their houses, then answer the questions below.

    a) What rooms are there in Pierre's house?
    b) Who has the most rooms in their house?
    c) Who has a dining room in their house?
    d) Who has a table in their bedroom?
    e) What things do **both** Pierre and Sophie have in their bedrooms?

Where You Live

Describing the kind of place you live in is a good, easy way to start up a conversation in French.

Tell them where you live — **J'habite...**

You need to learn the words for <u>flat</u> and <u>house</u>...

J'habite <u>dans</u>...

= I live in...

**a flat:
un appartement**

**a house:
une maison**

...and the words for <u>village</u>, <u>town</u> and <u>city</u>.

J'habite <u>dans</u>...

= I live in...

**a village:
un village**

**a town:
une ville**

**a big town / city:
une grande ville**

Some extra phrases

Here are some extra phrases you might find useful when talking about where you live:

J'habite <u>à la</u> campagne.   = I live in the countryside.

J'habite <u>à la</u> montagne.   = I live in the mountains.

J'habite <u>au bord de la</u> mer.   = I live by the sea.

This is useful stuff
If you speak to real people in French, you'll find that the first thing you end up telling them is where you live. It always happens. 'I live in a town called...' always comes up in conversation.

Where You Live

Here's how to give a few more details on where you live.

Tell them **exactly** where you live

Here's a nice long phrase to impress your teacher.

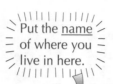
Put the name of where you live in here.

a *village:* un village
a *town:* une ville
a *big town/city:* une grande ville

J'habite à Kendal, une ville dans le nord-ouest de l'Angleterre.

= I live in Kendal, a town in the north-west of England.

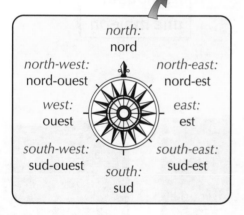

north: nord
north-west: nord-ouest
north-east: nord-est
west: ouest
east: est
south-west: sud-ouest
south-east: sud-est
south: sud

of Scotland: de l'Écosse
of Wales: du Pays de Galles
of Northern Ireland: de l'Irlande du Nord

Do you like living here? — **Tu aimes habiter ici?**

Learn these phrases and all the vocab.

J'aime habiter ici

= I like living here

Je n'aime pas habiter ici

= I don't like living here

...parce que c'est

= because it is

fantastic: fantastique
interesting: intéressant
quiet: tranquille

...parce que c'est

= because it is

terrible: terrible
boring: ennuyeux
too quiet: trop tranquille

Learn how to give plenty of detail about where you're from
These phrases are great ones to learn because they're fairly simple but also very useful. You can give quite a lot of info about where you live without getting muddled up in tricky grammar.

Daily Routines

What you do and when you do it — it won't make a good story, but it'll help you pass French.

Daily routine — say **what** you do

This is how you say all the simple things you do. Learn them <u>all</u>.

All these "Je me..." ones are <u>reflexive verbs</u> — see p.139-140.

I wake up:
Je me réveille.

I get up:
Je me lève.

I get dressed:
Je m'habille.

I wash myself:
Je me lave.

I brush my teeth:
Je me brosse les dents.

I eat breakfast:
Je prends le petit déjeuner.

I go to school:
Je vais à l'école.

(See p.84 for "by bus" etc.)

I go home:
Je rentre à la maison.

I do my homework:
Je fais mes devoirs.

I watch telly:
Je regarde la télé.

I eat dinner:
Je prends le dîner.

I go to bed:
Je me couche.

Get up, stand up, don't give up the fight
On the left hand side of a page write out all of these sentences in <u>English</u>. Translate them into <u>French</u> on the right of the page. <u>Cover</u> the English and translate them back. Fun, eh?

Daily Routines

When you're talking about daily routines, you need to be able to say when you do things.

Say when you do things — à 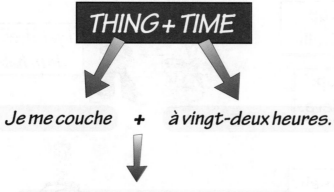 heures

Take the activities from the last page and add a <u>time</u> to say <u>when</u> you do them.
It's a <u>classic way</u> to turn your sentences from good to <u>impressive</u>.

THING + TIME

Je me couche **+** *à vingt-deux heures.*

Je me couche à vingt-deux heures.　　= I go to bed at ten o'clock.

Some **examples** to give you the idea

Je me lève à sept heures et demie.　　= I get up at 07:30.

Je vais à l'école à huit heures,
et je rentre à la maison à seize heures.　　= I go to school at 08:00,
and I go home at 16:00.

Je prends le dîner à dix-neuf heures.　　= I eat dinner at 19:00.

Je me couche à vingt-et-une heures.　　= I go to bed at 21:00.

'Vingt-et-un' becomes 'vignt-et-**une**' here
because 'heure' is feminine — see p.120.

Remember to use the 24-hour clock
The easiest mistake you can make with this stuff is forgetting to use the 24-hour clock.
You don't want to end up telling everyone that you go to bed at ten in the morning, eh?

Chores

Chores — the only thing less enjoyable than school work. Except pulling your own toenails out perhaps, but that's not something your mum makes you do after school. (I hope.)

Learn these phrases for **chores**

Here's how to tell people that you're doing certain <u>chores</u>.
<u>Learn</u> them all (and then get on with the washing up, and tidy your room, you dirty layabout).

Je passe l'aspirateur.   = I do the vacuum cleaning.

Je fais la vaisselle.   = I do the washing up.

Je range ma chambre.   = I tidy my room.

Je lave la voiture.   = I wash the car.

Je fais les courses.   = I do the shopping.

Je fais le ménage.   = I do the cleaning.

Je mets la table.   = I lay the table.

Je fais mon lit.   = I make my bed.

You might **not** have any **chores**

If you're lucky enough to have <u>no chores</u>, here's what you could say:

Je ne fais rien.   = I don't do anything.

And for your next chore, test yourself on all these phrases

It might not be much fun to chat about chores with your French pals, but these little phrases have verbs in that you're going to see again and again. So make sure you get to know them.

The Body

Here's an easy page to learn. Just look at the boxes and learn the words.

The body — Le corps

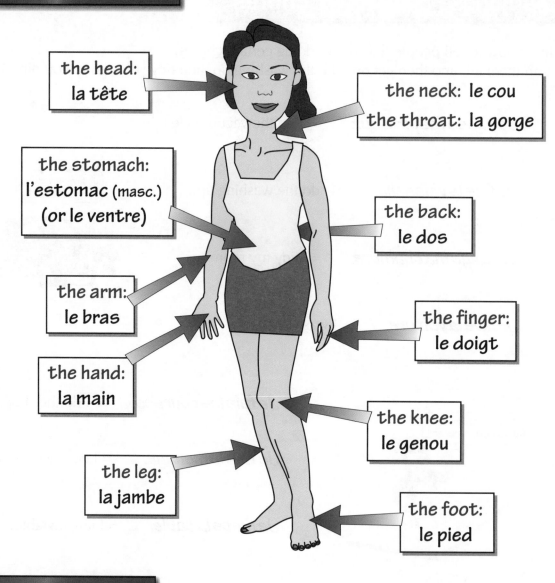

the head: la tête

the neck: le cou
the throat: la gorge

the stomach: l'estomac (masc.) (or le ventre)

the back: le dos

the arm: le bras

the finger: le doigt

the hand: la main

the knee: le genou

the leg: la jambe

the foot: le pied

The head — La tête

hair: les cheveux (masc.)

the eye: l'œil (masc.)
the eyes: les yeux

the ear: l'oreille (fem.)

the mouth: la bouche

the nose: le nez

the tooth: la dent

Useful for when you need to say which bit hurts

Learning the French for parts of the body is really useful for those occasions when you might need to tell a doctor which bits hurt. You could always point, but it's much nicer to speak.

Health and Illness

Say you're ill, explain what's wrong, and then ask for medicine. It's all on these two pages.

I'm ill — **Je suis malade**

This sentence is a <u>good one</u> to learn. You can go into <u>more detail</u> later.

Je suis malade. = I am ill.

Je veux aller chez le médecin. = I want to go to the doctor's.

> to the hospital: à l'hôpital
> to the chemist's: à la pharmacie

Learn these things for **making you better**

If you're ill, you'll need one of these things to make you <u>better</u>.

medicine: **un médicament**

a prescription: *une ordonnance*

an aspirin: **une aspirine**

tablets: *des comprimés*

a plaster: **un sparadrap**

cream: *de la crème*

Fingers crossed, you won't get sick if you go to France
Still, it's just as well to know how to say what the matter is, just in case. You don't dial 999 for an ambulance in France, by the way — it's 112. If you go there on holiday, don't forget that.

34

Health and Illness

If you're not feeling well, you need to be able to explain what's the matter.

My ... hurts — J'ai mal à ...

This is how you say <u>what bit</u> of you hurts.

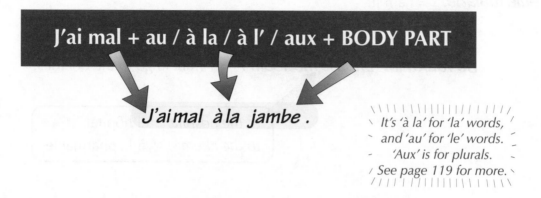

J'ai mal + au / à la / à l' / aux + BODY PART

J'ai mal à la jambe .

It's 'à la' for 'la' words, and 'au' for 'le' words. 'Aux' is for plurals. See page 119 for more.

You can use this phrase with **other body parts**

You can use the phrase you've just learnt with <u>most parts</u> of the body.
Practise using the words for body parts from p.32.

J'ai mal **au pied** .   = My foot hurts.

J'ai mal **à l'éstomac** .   = My stomach hurts (I have stomach ache).

J'ai mal **à la tête** .   = My head hurts (I have a headache).

J'ai mal **aux oreilles** .   = My ears hurt (I have earache).

You don't use special words for headache, earache or whatever. You just say which bit hurts.

So that's why you need to know if a word is 'le' or 'la'

If you don't know, you won't know whether to use 'au' or 'à la'. It's probably easiest to learn the ones on this page as whole phrases — that way at least you'll know the common ones.

Practice Questions

1   Write down in English where each of these people say they live.

a) J'habite dans un appartement.

b) J'habite dans une maison.

c) J'habite dans un village.

d) J'habite dans une ville.

e) J'habite dans une grande ville.

Track 6   Listening Question

2   Listen to what the French people say about where they live, and then decide whether the statements below (a-e) are true or false.

    a)   François likes living in Paris because it's interesting.
    b)   Marie doesn't like her village because it's too quiet.
    c)   Bordeaux is in the north of France.
    d)   Chantal thinks Strasbourg is exciting.
    e)   Both the boys like where they live.

---

3   Kevin has tried to describe his daily routine, but he's got it all in the wrong order. Copy out the sentences below in the right order. Then translate them into English.

Je me lave à sept heures et demie.

Je me couche à vingt-deux heures.

Je rentre à la maison à seize heures.

Je me réveille à sept heures.

À dix-sept heures je regarde la télé.

Je vais à l'école à huit heures et demie.

Je prends le dîner à vingt heures.

Je mange le petit déjeuner à huit heures.

---

4   In French, write out what these people say about their chores.

    a)   Kate: I wash the car and I do the vacuuming.

    b)   Brian: I wash the dishes and I do the shopping.

    c)   Kavita: I tidy my room and I make my bed.

    d)   Richard: I lay the table and I do the cleaning.

    e)   Thomas: I don't do anything.

Practice Questions

5 Look at the picture of the person below, and then choose words from the box on the right to match the labels A-J.

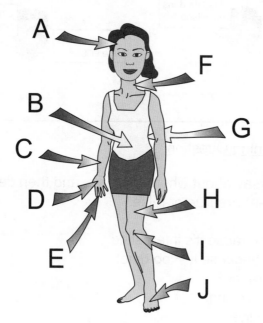

la main

le bras

le pied

l'estomac

la tête

le dos

le doigt

la jambe

le genou

le cou

6 Copy and complete each sentence below using **au**, **à l'**, **à la** or **aux**.

au	à l'	à la	aux

a) J'ai mal .... ventre.

b) J'ai mal .... oreilles.

c) J'ai mal .... dent.

d) J'ai mal .... gorge.

e) J'ai mal .... tête.

f) J'ai mal .... estomac.

Track 7 Listening Question

7 Listen to Jean and Marie talking about their illnesses, then answer the questions.

a) What is wrong with Jean?

b) Where does Jean want to go?

c) Who has toothache?

d) Who has the most problems?

e) What does Marie want to make her better?

Summary Questions

Congratulations, you've got to the end of the section. You've learnt how to tell people about yourself, your house, your daily routine and loads more. Or have you? Let's see...

1) Answer these questions, in French:
a) Comment tu t'appelles?   b) Quel âge as-tu?
c) Quelle est la date de ton anniversaire?

2) In French, give three details about what you look like.

3) What do these phrases mean?
a) Je suis sympa. b) Je suis sportif. c) Je suis paresseuse. d) Je suis timide.

4) How do you say these phrases in French?
a) I have a mother. b) I have a sister. c) My grandfather is called Wilbert.
d) My (female) cousin is called April. e) She is sixteen years old.

5) How do you say these in French? a) dog b) cat c) bird d) mouse e) hamster

6) What are these in English? a) le lapin b) la tortue c) le cheval d) la vache

7) Jean-Claude and Marie are talking about their pets. Jean-Claude says he has a cat, his cat's name is "Fluffy", and his cat is nasty. Marie says she doesn't have a pet. Write out their conversation in French.

8) Say this in French:
"In my home, there is a bathroom, a dining room and a garden."

9) Say how many rooms there are in your house (in French, of course).

10) Antoine is talking about his bedroom. What does this mean in English?
"Dans ma chambre, il y a une table, un placard, et une armoire."

11) In French, say that there's a chair, a bed and a sofa in your room.

12) What does this mean in English?
"J'habite dans un appartement. J'habite dans une grande ville.
J'habite à Londres, une grande ville dans le sud-est de l'Angleterre."

13) Jean-Claude and Marie are talking about where they live. Marie says, "I don't like living here because it's boring." Jean-Claude says, "I like living here because it's quiet." Write out their conversation in French.

14) Say these in English:
a) Je me lève à huit heures. b) Je vais à l'école à neuf heures.

15) Say these in French:
a) I get dressed.   b) I brush my teeth.   c) I eat dinner at 19:00.

16) Put the French chores into English, and the English chores into French:
a) Je passe l'aspirateur. b) I do the washing up. c) Je range ma chambre.
d) I wash the car. e) Je fais les courses. f) Je mets la table. g) I make my bed.

17) Write out this list of body parts in French:
head, arm, leg, hand, foot, nose, mouth, tooth.

18) You are at the doctor's in France. Say your head hurts, then say your leg hurts.

19) How do you tell someone that you're ill in French?
Write down the names of four things that could make you better.

School Subjects

Not only do you have to go to school, but now you have to talk about what you do there as well. It's all just standard Key Stage 3 French, I'm afraid.

School Subjects — Les matières

Make sure you can say all the subjects in French
— all the ones you do, and the ones you don't.

SCIENCE

science: les sciences
physics: la physique
chemistry: la chimie
biology: la biologie

HUMANITIES

history: l'histoire
geography: la géographie
religious studies: l'instruction religieuse

PHYSICAL EDUCATION

PE: l'éducation physique et sportive (EPS)

NUMBERS AND STUFF

maths: les maths
ICT: l'informatique

LANGUAGES

English: l'anglais
French: le français
German: l'allemand
Spanish: l'espagnol

ART AND MUSIC

art: le dessin
music: la musique

Je fais de l'histoire.   = I do history.

de + le = du
(see page 121 for more)

Je fais du dessin.   = I do art.

Je fais des maths.   = I do maths.

Why do you have to do so many subjects?

Well that's probably a question you're asking yourself every day already. Just learn the ones on this page, and if you do anything else weird that's not on the list, just look it up in a dictionary.

School Subjects

Now you've learnt the <u>names</u> of the subjects, you're ready to talk about them in more detail.

My favourite subject — **Ma matière préférée**

Use these phrases to show what you think about your subjects.

Ma matière préférée est + SUBJECT

Ma matière préférée est l'histoire   = My favourite subject is history.

J'aime l'histoire.   = I like history.

Je déteste l'histoire.   = I hate history.

Give a reason for your choice

Je déteste *l'histoire* *parce que c'est* *inutile* .

= I hate history because it's useless.

For more opinions, see pages 111-112.

interesting: intéressant
boring: ennuyeux
easy: facile
difficult: difficile
useful: utile
useless: inutile

If you don't have any opinions, it's time to get some

If you really want extra brownie points, you might want to say that French is your favourite subject. Seriously though, it doesn't matter what you say but it's good if you give a reason.

School Routine

For some reason, you need to be able to talk a lot about your <u>daily routine</u>.

The school day — La journée scolaire

Je vais à l'école en voiture *.* = I go to school by car.

> *by bus:* en bus
> *by bike:* en vélo
> *on foot:* à pied

For more on transport, see p.84

Je me lève à sept heures *.* = I get up at 7 o'clock.

For more times, see p. 3

For more on home routines, see p. 29

Les cours commencent à neuf heures *.* = Lessons begin at 9.00.

Les cours finissent à trois heures et demie *.* = Lessons end at 3.30.

Chaque cour dure quarante minutes *.* = Each lesson lasts 40 minutes.

Nous faisons une heure *de devoirs par jour.* = We do one hour of homework every day.

For more numbers, see p. 1

Just learn how to chat about your school day

You'll find out that things are a little bit different in French schools. For a start, their lessons begin at 8am. It makes having to get up for a 9am lesson seem a little bit easier, I reckon.

Classroom Stuff

Your teacher may actually give you some <u>instructions</u> in French when you're in the classroom. Learn these <u>handy phrases</u> so you can understand what they're shouting about.

Sit down! — Asseyez-vous!

Here are some of the things you may hear your French teacher shouting at the class:

Levez-vous! = Stand up!

Asseyez-vous! = Sit down!

Écoutez! = Listen!

Taisez-vous! = Shut up!

Use these phrases when you're stuck

Qu'est-ce que ça veut dire? = What does that mean?

Qu'est-ce que c'est en français? = What is that in French?

Qu'est-ce que c'est en anglais? = What is that in English?

And just in case you need to say '<u>true</u>' and '<u>false</u>'...

vrai = true   **faux** = false

This page can get you out of a lot of trouble

It's a typical scene in a French class — a lot of confused students, and the teacher's yelling random orders in French that no one understands. Well now you'll know what they're saying.

In the Classroom

This classroom vocabulary might come in really <u>useful</u>.

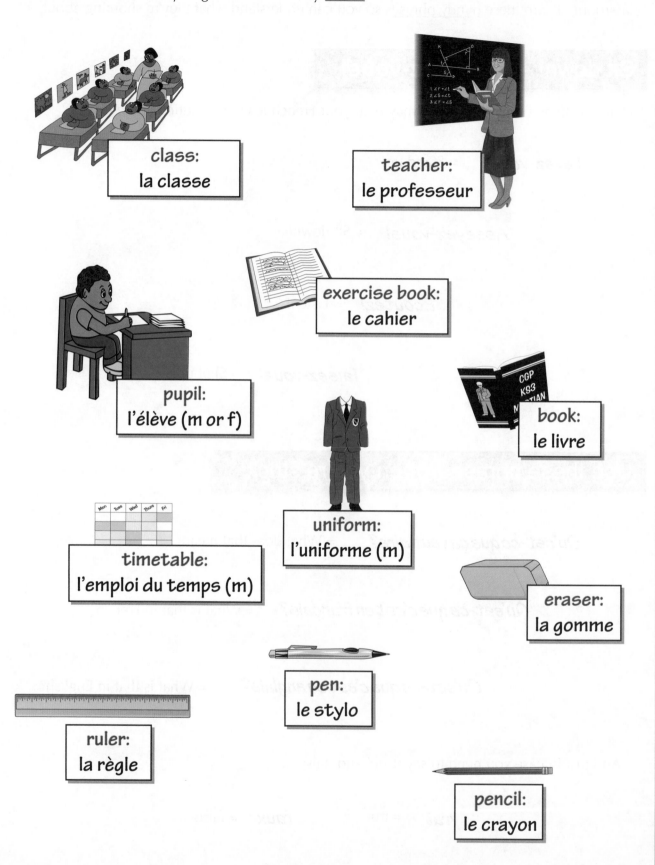

class:
la classe

teacher:
le professeur

pupil:
l'élève (m or f)

exercise book:
le cahier

book:
le livre

uniform:
l'uniforme (m)

timetable:
l'emploi du temps (m)

eraser:
la gomme

pen:
le stylo

ruler:
la règle

pencil:
le crayon

What a lovely page of vocabulary

Well OK, maybe it's not all that exciting. It's the sort of stuff that comes up in the classroom all the time, so it's worth learning these words. It'll help you talk about things at school, anyway.

Jobs

These are the <u>important jobs</u> you need to learn. They can crop up in your <u>listening</u> and <u>reading</u> tests. Make sure that you learn the jobs that your <u>family</u> do, or that <u>you</u> want to do.

builder:
👫 maçon

hairdresser:
👨 coiffeur
👩 coiffeuse

mechanic:
👨 mécanicien
👩 mécanicienne

actor:
👨 acteur
👩 actrice

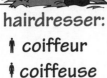

engineer:
👫 ingénieur

salesperson:
👨 vendeur
👩 vendeuse

Hope your favourite job's on this page

Obviously there wasn't room to include every job in the world, so we've just given you a few common ones. If your Gran's a lion tamer or something, then go and look it up in a dictionary.

Jobs

Here's some <u>more</u> jobs that often crop up in KS3 French.

secretary:
♂♀ secrétaire

office worker:
♂ employé de bureau
♀ employée de bureau

unemployed:
♂♀ au chômage

doctor:
♂♀ médecin

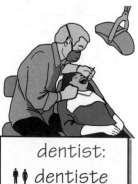

dentist:
♂♀ dentiste

vet:
♂♀ vétérinaire

policeman/woman:
♂♀ gendarme

nurse:
♂ infirmier
♀ infirmière

Here's another page of jobs

Here's a few more jobs that might come in handy. I realise that 'unemployed' isn't really a job, but it's here anyway, because it's jolly useful to know how to say it.

Talking about Jobs

There are <u>millions</u> of jobs. If the one that you want isn't on pages 43-44, then just choose the one that's nearest, or look it up in a <u>dictionary</u>, or just <u>pretend</u>.

Say what you do and what other people do

If you have a job, learn to say what you do, and what your parents do.

Je suis dentiste.   = I'm a dentist.   (This probably isn't true, but learn the French anyway.)

Je travaille chez 'Tile World'.   = I work at 'Tile World'.

Ma mère est vétérinaire.   = My mother is a vet.

Mon père est gendarme.   = My father is a policeman.

Remember, don't put 'un' or 'une' in front of these jobs. Just put 'suis' or 'est' and then the job.

I have a part-time job — J'ai un travail à mi-temps

If you're doing KS3 French, you're <u>probably not</u> a dentist yet.
You might need these phrases instead:

Je distribue des journaux.   = I deliver newspapers.

J'ai un travail à mi-temps.   = I have a part-time job.

Don't panic if you can't remember the name of a job
If the teacher asks you a question about your mum's job or something, then don't worry if you can't remember the name of it. You could always say where she works instead.

Talking about Jobs

This page is <u>pretty important.</u> It's all about saying what you want to do in the <u>future</u>, once you finally leave school.

I want to study... — Je veux étudier...

<u>First things first</u> — if you want to do some careers, you'll have to do a fair bit more <u>studying</u> before you get qualified. Here's how to talk about what you want to study at <u>GCSE</u>, <u>A-level</u>, or <u>beyond</u>.

> **Je veux étudier + SUBJECT**

Je veux étudier **les maths** . = I want to study maths.

See p. 38 for more subjects.

Give a <u>short reason</u> why you want to study that subject:

... parce que **c'est intéressant** . = ... because it's interesting.

> *c'est facile:* it's easy
> *c'est amusant:* it's fun
> *je veux être ingénieur:* I want to be an engineer

I want to be... — Je veux être...

> **Je veux être + JOB**

Je veux être **acteur** . = I want to be an actor.

You can use the reasons above, or you could use this one:

... parce qu'on gagne beaucoup d'argent. = ... because they earn a lot of money.

I love planning for the future
This is a sort of dream page, because you get to imagine life beyond KS3 French. Yes, once you wade your way through all those exams in the next few years, you can get a great job. Yay.

Practice Questions

Track 8   Listening Question

1   Listen to Marcel talking about his school subjects, then write down if each of the sentences below is true or false.

   a)   Marcel studies French.

   b)   Marcel says that he hates science.

   c)   Marcel likes English.

   d)   Marcel doesn't like maths.

   e)   Marcel's favourite subject is art.

2   Copy out and complete these sentences in French.
     The bits in brackets tell you what to say.

   a)   (I get up) .... à sept heures.

   b)   (I go to school) .... en vélo.

   c)   (Classes start) .... à huit heures et demie.

   d)   Je fais (one hour of homework) .... par jour.

3   Copy out the passage below and fill in the spaces with the correct words from the box.

Il y a 30 .... dans ma .... Le .... s'appelle

John Smith. J'écris les exercices dans mon .... avec un ....

Quand je fais une erreur je l'efface avec la .... L'anglais, c'est cool.

cahier	professeur	gomme	classe	crayon	élèves

Practice Questions

4   From the box below, choose the right person to do each job. With these jobs, it's the same word for a man or a woman. The first one has been done for you.

a)   This person helps build things.   Il/elle est ......*maçon*......... .

b)   This person looks after your teeth.   Il/elle est ....

c)   This person helps stop crime.   Il/elle est ....

d)   This person teaches in a school.   Il/elle est ....

e)   This person stops you being ill.   Il/elle est ....

f)   This person does a lot of typing and planning.   Il/elle est ....

gendarme	professeur	secrétaire	~~maçon~~
	médecin	dentiste	

5   Your penpal Charles sends you a letter telling you all about the work that he and his family do. Read the letter and answer the questions in English.

> *Je vais au collège. J'y vais à pied. Les cours commencent à 8h. Ma soeur, Dominique, travaille dans un bureau — elle est secrétaire, et mon frère, Didier, est vendeur chez Monsieur Bricolage. Mon père est dentiste, et ma mère a un travail à mi-temps — elle est coiffeuse. A l'avenir, je veux être ingénieur, parce que c'est très intéressant.*

a)   How does Charles get to school?

b)   What job does Dominique have?

c)   Is Pierre's brother an actor?

d)   Where does his brother work?

e)   Who is a dentist?

f)   What sort of job does his mother have?

g)   What does he want to do when he grows up?

Summary Questions

Well, this was never going to be a "laugh-a-minute" section, I suppose, what with all that school stuff in it. But you've come through smiling — well, you've come through it anyway. Now try answering all of these questions. Look up the answers to any you don't know, then try them again.

1) What subject(s) do you like? What don't you like? What is your favourite subject? Answer in French, and in full sentences.

2) Jean-Pierre goes to school by bus. Françoise goes on foot. How would each of them say how they get to school?

3) How do you say that you have five lessons each day?

4) Say that each lesson lasts 45 minutes, and that you have two hours of homework.

5) What do these mean? a) Écoutez! b) Asseyez-vous!

6) How do you say these in French? a) true b) false c) stand up! d) be quiet!

7) Your teacher is holding up an exercise book, and says "Qu'est-ce que c'est en français?" What would your answer be?

8) Say the French words for these things — out loud:
 a) pen b) rubber c) uniform d) book

9) What are these in English? a) l'élève b) le cahier c) la règle d) le crayon

10) How do you say these jobs in French? (Give both the male and female versions if they're different.)
 a) engineer b) actor c) policeman d) hairdresser e) teacher f) doctor

11) Say what jobs your parents do.

12) You have a part-time job at "House of Mango".
 Write down how you'd tell your French penfriend Jacques all about it.

13) I want to study chemistry, because I want to be a doctor.
 How would I say that in French?

14) What does this mean: "Je veux étudier l'histoire, parce que c'est intéressant."

15) How do you say this in French: "I want to be a hairdresser, because it's fun."

Directions

This section covers the three things <u>vital</u> to anyone's survival — <u>food</u>, <u>drink</u> and <u>shopping</u>. This page will help you to get to the shops in the first place, so it's an ideal place to start.

Where is...? — Où est...?

You need to learn <u>both</u> these phrases for 'Where's the...' so you can understand and use them. I've used '<u>la banque</u>' for the example — swap it for any place you like (see pages 52-54 for other places you might want to go to).

Où est la banque, s'il vous plaît?   = Where is the bank, please?

Pour aller à la banque, s'il vous plaît?   = How do you get to the bank, please?

Distances — ask if it's near or far

Don't go trekking off before you find out <u>how far it is</u>. Then you can get a bus instead.

C'est loin d'ici?   = Is it far from here?

Here are some of the answers you might get:

C'est près d'ici.   = It's near here.

C'est loin d'ici.   = It's far from here. (not terribly helpful)

C'est à dix kilomètres d'ici.   = It's 10km from here.

For other numbers, see page 1.

You'll need to learn this page in case you get lost

When you go on a French exchange, teachers have a nasty habit of letting you loose in a French town, and making you ask passers-by for directions, etc. Be prepared.

Directions

If someone asks you the way, you'll need to be able to tell them <u>where things are</u>. Or, more likely when you're in France, you'll need to <u>understand the directions you're given</u>.

You'll need to understand the directions you're given

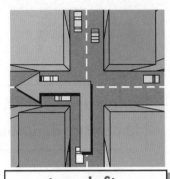

turn left:
tournez à gauche

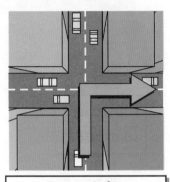

turn right:
tournez à droite

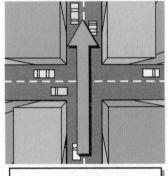

go straight on:
allez tout droit

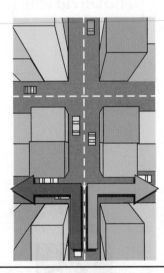

take the first street on the left / on the right:
prenez la première rue à gauche / à droite

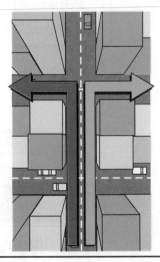

take the second street on the left / on the right:
prenez la deuxième rue à gauche / à droite

Teachers always ask you about this stuff

That's because it's really useful. When you're lost in Paris and the coach with the rest of the class on it is about to head home without you, you'll be glad you learnt these phrases.

Places in Town

This page has got the names of all those <u>big buildings</u> full of people that you find in big places. Learn them or you might find youself waiting days for a train in the local library.

museum:
le musée

train station:
la gare

leisure centre:
le centre de loisirs

bank:
la banque

town hall:
l'hôtel de ville (m)

park:
le parc

library:
la bibliothèque

cinema:
le cinéma

These are just some of the places you might want to go to

Obviously there are plenty of other places in a town that you might need to visit, but there isn't room to list them all here. If you learn these ones, you'll be off to a pretty good start.

Places in Town

Here are a few <u>more</u> places you might want to go to:

theatre:
le théâtre

tourist office:
le syndicat d'initiative
(l'office de tourisme)

town centre:
le centre-ville (m)

post office:
la poste

hotel:
l'hôtel (m)

swimming pool:
la piscine

palace/castle:
le château

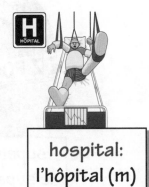
hospital:
l'hôpital (m)

cathedral:
la cathédrale

Even more vocabulary to learn

That's the thing about learning a foreign language — you can learn a few key phrases, but then you also have to learn the vocabulary to fit into those phrases, or you can't say very much.

Shops

Now learn the names of a few <u>shops</u> where you can go and spend your cash.

butcher's:
la boucherie

delicatessen:
la charcuterie

market:
le marché

baker's:
la boulangerie

bookshop:
la librairie

sweetshop:
la confiserie

chemist's:
la pharmacie

cake shop:
la pâtisserie

supermarket:
le supermarché

There's not too much to learn on this page
There are a couple of cheeky extra ones that you might like to learn: l'épicerie is the grocer's, and l'hypermarché is a hypermarket. That's like an absolutely massive supermarket, by the way.

Practice Questions

Listening Question

1 Listen to these four conversations where people are asking for directions.
Then write down whether the statement about each conversation is true or false.

a) The person wants to know where the bank is.

b) You should turn left to get to the supermarket.

c) The station is on the second street on the right.

d) The butcher's is 2 kilometres away.

2 You're on holiday in France, and your English friends are telling you what they want to do. Where do they need to go to do the following things? Write the name of the place in **French**.

a) I want to go swimming.

b) I want to see a film.

c) I want to buy some stamps.

d) I want to change some traveller's cheques.

e) I want to find out what there is to do in the town.

f) I want to catch a train to Angers.

3 Where would you buy the following items? Write the name of the shop in **French**.
Don't write down 'le supermarché' or 'l'hypermarché' — that's cheating.

a) bread

b) cake

c) a dictionary

d) aspirin

e) a lamb chop

f) salami

Fruit and Vegetables

This is a lovely page, packed full of <u>vitamin C</u>. Don't worry — <u>chips</u> are on page 57.

Fruit — les fruits

['le fruit' = fruit]

apple:
la pomme

orange:
l'orange (f)

lemon:
le citron

banana:
la banane

pear:
la poire

peach:
la pêche

strawberry:
la fraise

Vegetables — les légumes

['le légume' = vegetable]

peas:
les petits-pois

mushroom:
le champignon

potato:
la pomme de terre

tomato:
la tomate

French bean:
le haricot vert

carrot:
la carotte

lettuce:
la salade

onion:
l'oignon (m)

cauliflower:
le chou-fleur

This is the healthiest page in the whole book

This page looks just like a greengrocer's shop. If you don't like green things, you'd best move straight on to the next page. Seriously though, you do need to learn this food vocabulary.

Meat and Stodge

This page has most of the <u>meat</u> and '<u>stodge</u>' words that you're likely to want.

Meat — la viande

beef:
le bœuf

pork:
le porc

lamb:
l'agneau (m)

chicken:
le poulet

steak:
le steak

ham:
le jambon

sausage:
la saucisse

salami-type sausage:
le saucisson

fish:
le poisson

seafood:
les fruits de mer

And now for the **stodge**...

OK, the hardest bit here is <u>chips</u> and <u>crisps</u>. The French for crisps is "les chips", which can get <u>dead confusing</u>.

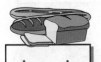

bread:
le pain

pasta:
les pâtes

cereal:
les céréales

rice:
le riz

chips:
les pommes frites

crisps:
les chips

Desserts and Dairy Products

Dessert — **le dessert**

jam:
la confiture

chocolate:
le chocolat

biscuit:
le biscuit

sugar:
le sucre

ice cream:
la glace

cake:
le gâteau

Learn these dairy products too

milk:
le lait

egg:
l'oeuf (m)

butter:
le beurre

yoghurt:
le yaourt

cream:
la crème

cheese:
le fromage

And now, the tastiest page in the whole book

These are definitely the most important words that you'll ever have to learn. If you learn just one thing in French, make sure it's how to order a choc-chip ice cream. It's vital stuff.

Drinks

Learning all that food vocabulary is <u>thirsty work</u>, so learn these words for drinks:

Drinks — **les boissons**

mineral water:
l'eau minérale (f)

cola:
le coca

orange juice:
le jus d'orange

Use <u>any fruit vocab</u> from p. 56 to make <u>any juice</u>. For example:

apple juice:
le jus de pomme

Hot drinks — **les boissons chaudes**

soup:
la soupe

hot chocolate:
le chocolat chaud

tea:
le thé

coffee:
le café

Learn these alcoholic drinks as well

white wine:
le vin blanc

red wine:
le vin rouge

beer:
la bière

You should have most of the words you'll need

If we haven't included the word for your favourite food or drink, you can always look it up in the dictionary. That's what they're for. But this little lot should be enough to get you started.

Talking about Food

You can switch your brain back on now, and use some of those words you've been learning.

I like — J'aime

Use 'j'aime' and 'je n'aime pas' to talk about anything you like or dislike.

J'aime *les pommes* . = I like apples.

See pages 111-112 for more on opinions.
See pages 56-59 for the names of foods.

bananas: les bananes
cream: la crème

Je n'aime pas *les légumes* . = I don't like vegetables.

peas: les petits pois
coffee: le café

Je suis *végétarien(ne)* . = I'm vegetarian.

vegan: végétalien(ne)

Don't say you're hungry, say you have hunger

Est-ce que tu as *faim* **?** = Are you hungry?

thirsty: soif

Oui, j'ai *faim* . = Yes, I'm hungry.

thirsty: soif

Non, je n'ai pas *faim* . = No, I'm not hungry.

People are definitely going to ask you these questions

'I don't like snails' is 'Je n'aime pas les escargots' by the way. They're supposed to be chewy and garlicky, apparently. But don't panic, as chances are you won't be offered any, anyway.

Mealtimes

Learn how to talk about what you <u>usually eat</u> at different times of the day.

Learn the words for mealtimes

breakfast:
le petit déjeuner

lunch:
le déjeuner

evening meal:
le dîner

Je mange... = I eat...

Je bois... = I drink...

Le petit déjeuner est à huit heures. Je mange des céréales. Le déjeuner est à douze heures. Je bois du lait. Le dîner est à dix-neuf heures. Je mange des pommes de terre.

= Breakfast is at 8 o'clock. I eat cereal. Lunch is at 12 o'clock. I drink milk. Dinner is at 7 o'clock. I eat potatoes.

French mealtimes can be a bit different from ours

French kids don't usually take a packed lunch — they often eat in the canteen, and the food's pretty good. They still like to go out for a burger and fries occasionally, though.

At a Restaurant

French people <u>eat out</u> quite a lot, in general. And the food's usually <u>great</u>.

Here's some handy restaurant vocabulary

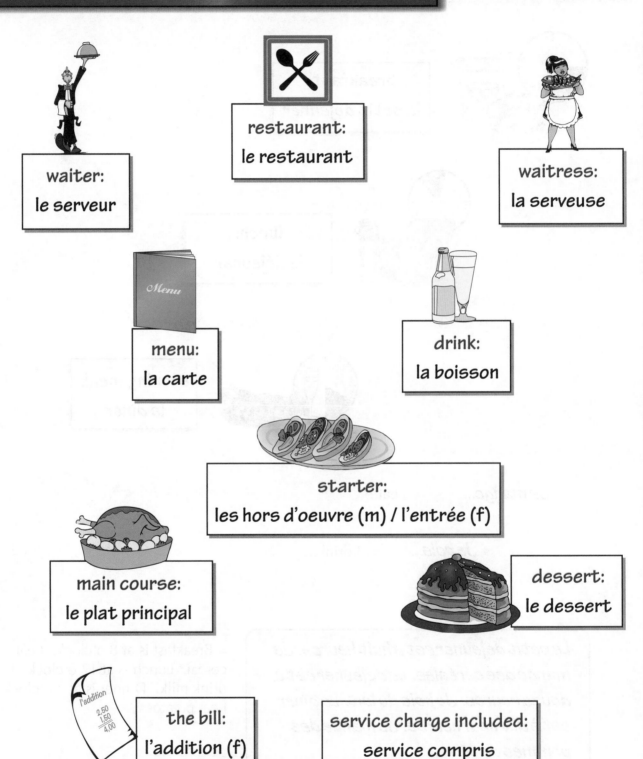

waiter:
le serveur

restaurant:
le restaurant

waitress:
la serveuse

menu:
la carte

drink:
la boisson

starter:
les hors d'oeuvre (m) / l'entrée (f)

main course:
le plat principal

dessert:
le dessert

the bill:
l'addition (f)

service charge included:
service compris

That's all you need to get you started

There aren't many Indian restaurants in France, so instead of going for a curry, they're more likely to go to a North African restaurant and get a 'cous-cous' instead. They're pretty spicy...

At a Restaurant

OK, you should have all the <u>vocabulary</u> you need, so now it's time to go to a restaurant.

Get yourself a **table**

Je voudrais réserver une table.   = I would like to reserve a table.

Une table pour deux personnes, s'il vous plaît.   = A table for two, please.

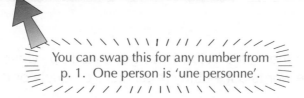

You can swap this for any number from
p. 1. One person is 'une personne'.

What would you like? — **Vous désirez?**

Once the waiter has asked you what you'd like, it's time to start ordering:

Avez-vous des steaks?   = Do you have steak?

Je voudrais un steak .   = I would like a steak.

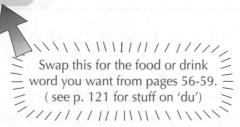

Swap this for the food or drink
word you want from pages 56-59.
(see p. 121 for stuff on 'du')

Ask for the **bill**

L'addition, s'il vous plaît.   = The bill, please.

Now put it all into practice

Try this role play with a mate, or a parent acting as the waiter — ask for a table for two, order
two different main courses and two drinks, then ask for the bill before you leave.

Practice Questions

1   Write out the words from the box under the correct heading — **fruit**, **vegetables** or **meats**.

le porc	l'oignon	la carotte
le champignon	la fraise	la saucisse
le saucisson	le poulet	la pêche
le chou-fleur	la poire	la pomme

2   The letters in the words below have got mixed up. Unscramble the letters and write the words out — they're all dairy products or desserts.

a)   al rmèec

b)   el rueber

c)   el utayor

d)   l'foue

e)   le situbci

f)   al ftureconi

g)   le cures

h)   el ocalthco

i)   el teuâga

j)   le mfragoe

Track 10   Listening Question

3   Amélie is asking you to do some shopping for her. Listen to what she is asking you to buy, then write down her shopping list in English, choosing the items from the box below.

rice	crisps	biscuits	milk
sugar	cake	sausages	cheese
cream	mushrooms	ice cream	apples
potatoes	ham	orange juice	a lemon

Practice Questions

4   How would you say these sentences in French?

a)   I like bananas.

b)   I don't like coffee.

c)   I am vegetarian.

d)   I don't like cream.

  Track 11   Listening Question

5   Listen to Isabelle talking about her meals and what she eats,
then answer the questions below.

a)   At what time does Isabelle eat breakfast?

b)   What does Isabelle eat for her evening meal?

c)   At which meal does she eat a sandwich?

---

6   Copy out these sentences, then fill in the gaps, choosing words from the box.

a)   Je voudrais .... une table .... quatre personnes,

s'il vous ....

b)   Vous .... ?

c)   Avez-vous .... ?

d)   Je .... de l'eau minérale.

e)   Je voudrais .... , s'il .... plaît.

désirez	du steak	voudrais	vous
plaît	réserver	pour	l'addition

Clothes

You'll often be asked to describe what someone's <u>wearing</u>:

Clothes — **les vêtements**

man's shirt:
la chemise

blouse:
le chemisier

trousers:
le pantalon

T-shirt:
le tee-shirt

jumper:
le pull

dress:
la robe

skirt:
la jupe

coat:
le manteau

waterproof coat:
l'imperméable (m)

hat:
le chapeau

glasses:
les lunettes

shoe:
la chaussure

sock:
la chaussette

glove:
le gant

tie:
la cravate

Say what you wear

It's all very well learning the vocabulary, but you need to know how to string a sentence together too:

Je porte + un / une / des + CLOTHES

It's '<u>un</u>' for '<u>le</u>' things, '<u>une</u>' for '<u>la</u>', and '<u>des</u>' if it's more than one. See pages 120-121.

Je porte une chemise.   = I'm wearing a shirt.

What are you wearing right now?
List the things that you're wearing. It'll help you to learn the vocabulary. This sort of stuff comes in really useful. And it'll be particularly useful if you go clothes shopping in France.

Colours and Materials

Now push your clothes descriptions up a gear by saying what <u>colour</u> they are.

Colours — les couleurs

black:
noir(e)

grey:
gris(e)

white:
blanc(he)

red:
rouge

yellow:
jaune

green:
vert(e)

blue:
bleu(e)

pink:
rose

orange:
orange

brown:
brun(e)

un tee-shirt *blanc* = a white T-shirt

The colour goes <u>after</u> the clothes word. Add the bit in brackets if it's a 'la' word.

Say what it's made of

wool:
la laine

cotton:
le coton

leather:
le cuir

une chemise *en coton* = a cotton shirt

The material goes <u>after</u> the clothes word. Don't forget that little word 'en'.

Describe your uniform

You might be asked to describe what you wear to school:

Je porte un pantalon gris, un pull en laine, une cravate noire, et une chemise en coton.

I wear grey trousers, a woollen sweater, a black tie and a cotton shirt.

This comes in handy when you're writing to your penfriend
Your French penfriend may not care what colour your uniform is, or that your jumper's made of wool, but just tell them anyway, because it's really good practice for all that vocabulary.

Asking for Stuff

This is the clothes shopping page. You can <u>buy stuff</u> using these phrases. Handy.

Je voudrais...

Je voudrais une jupe .   = I would like a skirt.

Avez-vous une jupe .   = Do you have a skirt?

Stick 's'il vous plaît' on the end of these to make them more polite.

Autre chose?   = Anything else?

C'est tout?   = Is that all?

Oui, s'il vous plaît.   = Yes please.

Non, merci.   = No thank you.

Je le/la prends.   = I'll take it.

Je ne le/la prends pas.   = I won't take it.

This is a direct object pronoun —
see p.123.

There are a lot of important things here

It's a good idea to practise putting these phrases together by acting out a pretend conversation with a friend. That way you're more likely to remember the right phrase when you need it.

Prices

At some point, if you really want that top you're going to have to <u>pay for it</u> — here's how:

Ask how much things cost

Ça coûte combien ?   = How much does it cost?

C'est combien?   = How much is it?

Ça fait combien?   = How much does that come to?

French money is in Euros

Like most of Europe, France uses the euro. How convenient.
There are <u>100 cents</u> in a <u>euro</u>, like there are 100 pence in a pound.

This is what you'd <u>see</u> on a French <u>price tag</u>.
They use a <u>comma</u>, not a decimal point:

This is how you <u>say</u> the price: *Cinq euros et cinquante centimes*

This is the euro symbol.

This is why you need to know your numbers
If you can't remember them, look back at page 1 right now, before you go any further. If you're confident about numbers, you shouldn't have too much trouble with understanding prices.

Practice Questions

1 Write these sentences out in **French**:

a)   I wear a red dress.

b)   Pierre wears a leather coat.

c)   She wears a green blouse.

d)   He wears a grey waterproof coat.

e)   Thierry wears a woollen jumper.

f)   You wear a pink T-shirt.

g)   We wear black coats.

2 The following prices are all in euros. Write them out in French.

a)   €1,70   b)   €2,35

c)   €5,85   d)   €10,12

3 These phrases can all be used when shopping for clothes.
Write them out in **English**.

a)   Je la prends.

b)   C'est tout?

c)   Ça coûte combien?

Track 12   Listening Question

4 Amandine has gone clothes shopping. Listen to this conversation, then answer the questions below in **English**.

a)   What colour skirt does Amandine want?

b)   What other item of clothing does she want?

c)   How much is her total bill?

Summary Questions

This is the part you've been waiting for — where you find out what you've learnt, and what you need to go over again.

1) How do you say "Where is the cinema?" in French? Write down two ways.

2) What are these in English?
   a) tournez à droite   b) prenez la deuxième rue à gauche   c) allez tout droit

3) What are the French names for these shops? (Don't forget "le" and "la")
   a) grocer's   b) sweet shop   c) bookshop   d) supermarket   e) chemist's

4) Write down the English names for these shops:
   a) la boulangerie   b) la boucherie   c) le marché   d) la pâtisserie

5) What are these places called in English?
   a) le musée   b) la poste   c) la piscine   d) l'église   e) le syndicat d'initiative

6) ...And what are these places called in French?
   a) leisure centre   b) park   c) theatre   d) town centre   e) train station   f) bank

7) Write down the French names for each of these foods:
   a)   b)   c)   d)   e)   f)   g)

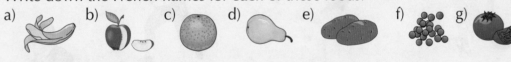

8) Name four vegetables, and write down what they are in French.

9) What are these drinks in English?
   apple juice, tea, white wine, hot chocolate, coffee, beer

10) In French, complete this phrase for four of the foods in question 7: "I like ..."
    Then say that you don't like each of the other three.

11) How do you ask someone if they are a) hungry, b) thirsty, and how would they say yes and no?

12) Write this out in French: "Breakfast is at 9 o'clock. Lunch is at 1 o'clock. Dinner is at 8 o'clock".

13) Put the French words into English, and the English into French:
    a) the bill   b) drink   c) le serveur   d) main course   e) les hors d'œuvre

14) Sven is at a French restaurant, in France. I've written out what he said in English. You write it in French.
    Sven: "A table for three people please." Waiter: *"What would you like?"*
    Sven: "I'd like the soup please."

Sports

Ah yes, <u>hobbies</u>, and <u>pastime</u> stuff. A classic bit of Key Stage Three French.

Learn the sports — **Les sports**

These are the <u>sports</u> you need to <u>know</u>. Lucky for you, most are <u>pretty similar</u> to the <u>English</u>.
(OK, so <u>chess</u> isn't a sport, but it's something that you might say you <u>play</u>.)

football:
le football

tennis:
le tennis

table tennis:
le tennis de table

badminton:
le badminton

cricket:
le cricket

rugby:
le rugby

chess:
les échecs

Say what you play — **Je joue ...**

"Je joue" + "au /à la /aux" + SPORT

Je joue au football.

It's "au" for "le" sports,
"à la" for "la", and "aux"
for "les" sports. See p.119

= I play football.

Sports — more fun than learning French at least

There are quite a few pages to learn on hobbies and stuff. I know it's unlikely that you play
badminton, chess and the clarinet, but pretend you do, just for the sake of learning French.

Musical Instruments

A useful page for musical ones among you. But non-musical ones have to learn it anyway.

Learn the instruments — Les instruments

You've got to know all of these, especially any that <u>you</u> actually play.

clarinet:
la clarinette

trumpet:
la trompette

piano:
le piano

guitar:
la guitare

drum kit:
la batterie

flute:
la flûte

violin:
le violon

cello:
le violoncelle

Say what you play — Je joue ...

"Je joue" + "du /de la /des" + INSTRUMENT

Je joue de la guitare.

= I play the guitar.

It's "du" for "le" instruments, "de la" for "la", and "des" for "les" instruments. See p.121

If you don't play an instrument, say you do anyway

Don't go to sleep yet — that's not all on the pastimes. There's a whole page of other random hobbies, and then you're going to get to learn how to say what you do and don't like.

Pastimes and Hobbies

This is about all those other hobbies where we say 'I go *something*-ing' or 'I do *something*'.

More activities — **Je fais de ...**

"<u>Je fais de</u> [...]" is a nice handy tool — you can use it for all of these activities:

cycling:
le cyclisme

swimming:
la natation

hiking:
les randonnées

skiing:
le ski

ice skating:
le patinage

shopping:
le shopping

Say what you do — **Je fais ...**

"Je fais" + "du /de la /des" + ACTIVITY

Je fais du cyclisme.

= I go cycling.

It's "du" for "le" activities, "de la" for "la", and "des" for "les" activities. See p.121

Je fais du homework
There must be something here that you enjoy doing. Even if there's not, learn all the names of the activities anyway and practise saying that you do them. (In *French*, obviously...)

Give Your Opinion

This is where you get to comment on all the hobbies and activities on the last few pages. So if you really hate or love football, for example, you can now tell people about it.

Say what you **do** and **don't like**

I've used just "le football" as an <u>example</u> here — you can <u>swap it</u> for any of the <u>sports</u> from page 72 or the <u>activities</u> from page 74 (e.g. J'aime la natation).

Est-ce que tu aimes le football?

= Do you like football?

J'aime le football.

= I like football.

Je n'aime pas le football.

= I don't like football.

J'adore le football.

= I love football.

Je déteste le football.

= I hate football.

...parce que c'est facile.

= because it's easy.

...parce que c'est difficile.

= because it's difficult.

fun: amusant
interesting: intéressant

boring: ennuyeux
tiring: fatigant

Je fais du staying in bed

"Est-ce que tu aimes..." (do you like...) is tricky because you don't pronounce all the bits. Say it now: *"ess ker tu em..."*. Now close the book and write it down spelt right. And again...

TV and Radio

Finally — an admission that there's nothing as good as <u>lounging about</u>.
Learn these phrases for things you can do in your <u>pyjamas</u>.

I watch television — **Je regarde la télévision**

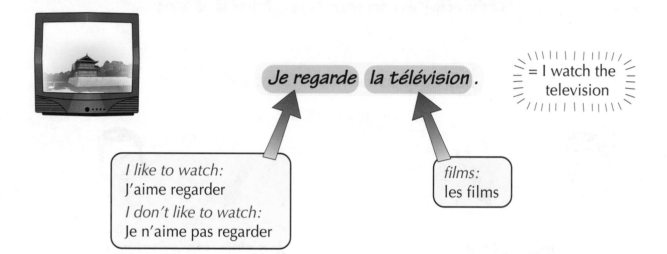

Je regarde   la télévision .

= I watch the television

I like to watch:
J'aime regarder
I don't like to watch:
Je n'aime pas regarder

films:
les films

I listen to the radio — **J'écoute la radio**

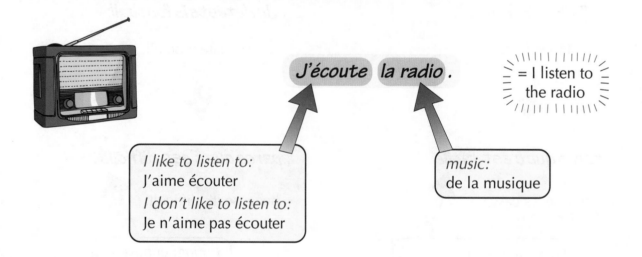

J'écoute   la radio .

= I listen to the radio

I like to listen to:
J'aime écouter
I don't like to listen to:
Je n'aime pas écouter

music:
de la musique

You can only regarde la télévision when you've learnt these
This is such an easy page. The words for TV, radio, music and films are pretty much the same as in English, and apart from that, you only have to learn 'j'écoute' and 'je regarde'. So easy.

Books and Opinions

Reading stuff is something else that you can do in your pyjamas. Here's how to tell people that you like to read, and also how to give your opinion on films, music, books, or whatever.

I read books — **Je lis des livres**

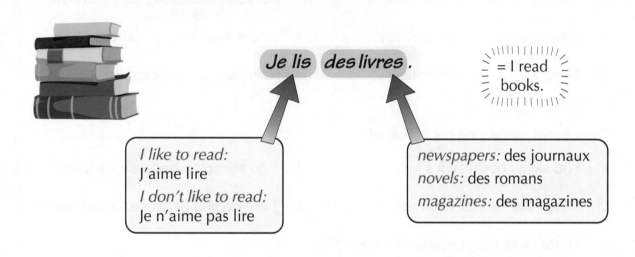

Je lis des livres .

I like to read:
J'aime lire

I don't like to read:
Je n'aime pas lire

= I read books.

newspapers: des journaux
novels: des romans
magazines: des magazines

I like this film — **J'aime ce film**

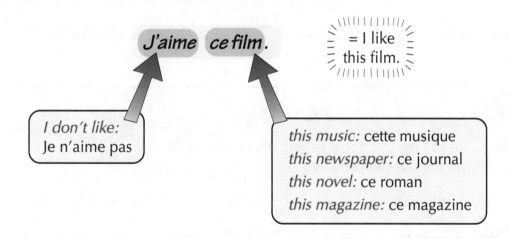

J'aime ce film .

I don't like:
Je n'aime pas

= I like this film.

this music: cette musique
this newspaper: ce journal
this novel: ce roman
this magazine: ce magazine

Books are great — even this one
Reading the telly, watching the radio and listening to books, ain't life grand... You might have noticed this is a pretty easy bit to learn. <u>Bad news</u> — you've got no excuse. <u>Learn it all</u>.

Practice Questions

1 Copy out and complete the sentences below, adding
de la / du / des, or **au / à la / aux**, whichever is correct.

a) Moi, je joue .... batterie.

b) Roger, il joue .... guitare.

c) Claude, il joue .... violoncelle.

d) Monique, elle joue .... clarinette.

e) Juliette joue .... badminton.

f) Vladimir joue .... échecs.

g) Miles joue .... trompette.

h) Ravi joue .... violon.

2 Write these sentences out in French.

a) I go skiing because it's fun.

b) I go shopping because it's easy.

c) I don't like football because it's difficult.

d) I like cycling because it's interesting.

e) I hate swimming because it's boring.

3 Answer the questions below with sentences, using **ce** or **cette**. A tick means you
like it, a cross means you don't. The first one has been done for you.

a) Est-ce que tu aimes le film? ✔ *Oui, j'aime ce film.*

b) Est-ce que tu aimes le film? ✘

c) Est-ce que tu aimes le roman? ✔

d) Est-ce que tu aimes le magazine? ✘

e) Est-ce que tu aimes le journal? ✘

f) Est-ce que tu aimes la musique? ✔

g) Est-ce que tu aimes le livre? ✔

Track 13 Listening Question

4 Listen to these French people talking about their hobbies,
then answer the questions below.

a) Who reads books?

b) Who listens to the radio?

c) Who doesn't like films?

d) Who doesn't read novels?

e) Who listens to music?

f) Who watches films?

g) Who doesn't like newspapers?

h) Who doesn't like television?

Going Out and Making Arrangements

It's all very well learning how to say 'I like reading', but it's a lot more useful to learn how to say 'Would you like to go to the cinema?' to those stunning French exchange students.

Learn the names of these **places to go**

You need to know the names of <u>places to go</u>.
Here's the <u>seven main ones</u>. For more places, see pages 52-54.

swimming pool:
la piscine

cinema:
le cinéma

theatre:
le théâtre

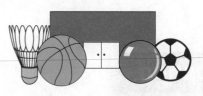

leisure centre:
le centre de loisirs

town centre:
le centre-ville

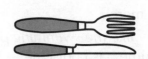

restaurant:
le restaurant

my place / your place:
chez moi / chez toi

Yes, *there's more vocabulary to learn*

OK, so this page might not have been very helpful for asking out attractive French visitors to your school, but it's a start. The next page will be much more helpful, I promise.

Going Out and Making Arrangements

This is the crucial bit. Now you can ask people out and know when you're being asked out.

Let's go... — **Allons...**

Here's how you <u>suggest</u> going to places:

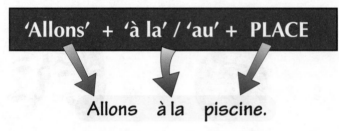

'Allons' + 'à la' / 'au' + PLACE

Allons   à la   piscine.

= Let's go to the swimming pool.

> It's 'au' for 'le' words and 'à la' for 'la' words. See p.119

<u>'Chez moi'</u> is the <u>odd one out</u>. You <u>don't</u> put the 'à la' / 'au' with 'chez' — just say <u>'allons chez moi'</u>.

Say yes or no to going out — **Oui** or **non**

If somebody asks you out, you might want to say <u>yes</u>, or you might want to say <u>no</u>. Here's how to do both:

'YES' PHRASES

Yes, OK:
Oui, d'accord.
Yes, I'd love to:
Oui, je veux bien.
Yes, good idea:
Oui, bonne idée.

'NO' PHRASES

No, thank you:
Non, merci.
I don't like the swimming pool:
Je n'aime pas la piscine.
I don't have any money:
Je n'ai pas d'argent.
I'm doing my homework:
Je fais mes devoirs.

You can only go to the cinema when you've done your homework
Make sure you've <u>learnt</u> those phrases — cover the <u>English</u> with your hand, then scribble down what the <u>French</u> means. Then <u>check</u> you got it right. <u>Keep at it</u> till you get them <u>all</u> right.

Going Out and Making Arrangements

More about going out — this time you're learning the details on <u>where and when to meet</u>.

When shall we meet? — On se retrouve quand?

Be specific...

On se retrouve *à huit heures*.

= Let's meet at eight o'clock.

at ten o'clock: à dix heures
at midday: à midi
at eight o'clock in the evening: à vingt heures

You can stick any <u>clock times</u> in here — see p.3.

Or be vague...

On se retrouve *ce soir*.

= Let's meet tonight.

this afternoon: cet après-midi
tomorrow: demain
on Monday: lundi

For <u>days of the week</u> see p.4.

Where shall we meet? — On se retrouve où?

On se retrouve *au cinéma*.

= Let's meet at the cinema.

The new word here is '<u>devant</u>' — 'in front of'.

at the swimming pool: à la piscine
in front of the swimming pool: devant la piscine
at my place: chez moi

Remember — it's 'au' for 'le' words and 'à la' for 'la' words. See p.119.

Practise these phrases over and over

Try out some combinations of the things you've learned. Suggest meeting yourself in front of the leisure centre at seven in the evening. And then say you can't because you've no money.

Going Out and Making Arrangements

The last thing you have to learn about going out is <u>buying tickets</u>. And then you can have fun.

Buying tickets — **billets**

Ticket buying is <u>essential</u> for the <u>cinema</u> and <u>theatre</u>.

Un billet coûte combien?

= How much does a ticket cost?

Un billet coûte deux euros.

= A ticket costs two euros.

Je voudrais un billet, s'il vous plaît. = I would like a
ticket please.

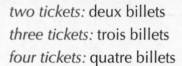

> *two tickets:* deux billets
> *three tickets:* trois billets
> *four tickets:* quatre billets

Put it all together

Look back over the last few pages, and make sure you can put <u>all</u>
the phrases <u>together</u>. <u>Test yourself</u> by putting this lot into <u>French</u>:

'Let's go to the cinema.'	*'Yes, good idea.'*
'When shall we meet?'	*'Let's meet at seven in the evening.'*
'Where shall we meet?'	*'Let's meet in front of the cinema.'*

Preferring to sneak in the fire exit is no excuse not to learn this
The best way to learn this stuff is simply to practise it loads. Have little conversations with
people about where to meet and what to do. And don't mix up your 'à la' with your 'au'.

Transport

You're going to need to know what buses and trains are called in French if you're ever going to travel by bus or train. In France, obviously.

Learn the names of these **vehicles**

car:
la voiture

train:
le train

boat:
le bateau

bus:
l'autobus (m)

bicycle:
le vélo

coach:
le car

aeroplane:
l'avion (m)

motorbike:
la moto

underground:
le métro

Learn these words before you move on to the next pages

Don't mix up 'car', 'voiture' and 'autobus'. '<u>Car</u>' = <u>coach</u>, '<u>voiture</u>' = <u>car</u> and '<u>autobus</u>' = <u>bus</u>. Get them clear in your head now. With the others, make sure you spell them exactly right.

Transport

'Ugg, me, train' isn't good enough for KS3 French — you need these phrases instead.

I go by... — **Je vais en**...

This is really useful stuff. It comes in handy when you're talking about <u>going out</u>, <u>going to school</u> and <u>holidays</u>.

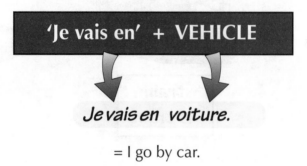

'Je vais en' + VEHICLE

Je vais en voiture.

= I go by car.

Use this for <u>any</u> of the transport types from p.83.
Here are the <u>four most common</u> ones:

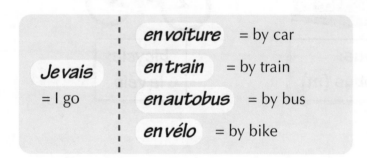

Je vais = I go	*en voiture* = by car
	en train = by train
	en autobus = by bus
	en vélo = by bike

There's a special phrase for <u>going on foot</u>:

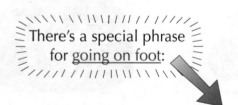

Je vais à pied. = I go on foot.

If you go by unicycle or balloon, you'll have to look that up yourself
Notice that for all the vehicles, you say 'je vais en', but when you're going on foot, you say 'je vais à'. There's no such thing as 'je vais en pied' so don't go making that mistake.

Transport

Now it's time to learn about buying train and bus tickets. Goody — everyone likes a trip out.

Use the **same phrases** for **train** and **bus tickets**

France has good trains that <u>actually work</u>, if you can imagine that.
There's a few phrases to learn here, but it's <u>essential stuff</u> for buying tickets.

Est-ce qu'il y a un train pour Lyon?   = Is there a train to Lyon?

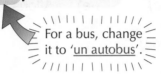
For a bus, change
it to '<u>un autobus</u>'.

TYPES OF TICKET

single: aller simple	return: aller-retour	first class: première classe	second class: deuxième classe

EXAMPLE: *Je voudrais un aller simple pour Lyon, première classe.*

= I would like a single to Lyon, 1st class.

Here are some **questions** you may need to use

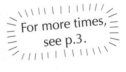
For a bus, change
it to '<u>l'autobus</u>'.

Q: À quelle heure part/arrive le train pour Lyon?

= What time does the train to Lyon leave/arrive?

For more times,
see p.3.

A: Le train pour Lyon part/arrive à dix heures.

= The train to Lyon leaves/arrives at ten o'clock.

Q: Le train pour Lyon part de quel quai?   = Which platform does the train to Lyon leave from?

A: Le train pour Lyon part du quai numéro deux.   = The train to Lyon leaves from platform two.

Learn your transport — but don't get carried away

Make sure you've got it sussed — <u>test yourself</u> by rewriting this <u>in French</u> (answer below):
'Is there a train to St. Malo? I would like a return, first class. What time does the train leave?'

ANSWER: Est-ce qu'il y a un train pour St. Malo? Je voudrais un aller- retour, première classe. À quelle heure part le train?

Practice Questions

1 These sentences are all suggestions to go somewhere.
Copy and complete them by writing the French for the place in brackets.
Remember to add **à la**, **au**, or **chez**. The first one has been done for you.

    a) Allons .... *[town centre]*   *Allons au centre-ville.*

    b) Allons .... *[swimming pool]*   c) Allons .... *[restaurant]*

    d) Allons .... *[my place]*   e) Allons .... *[cinema]*

    f) Allons .... *[your place]*

2 Translate the following responses into French.

    a) No thanks, I have no money.   b) Yes, I'd love to.

    c) No, I'm doing my homework.   d) No thanks, I don't like the leisure centre.

    e) Yes, good idea — I love the cinema.

3 These friends can't agree about where and when to meet.
Write in English what each one's suggesting.

    a) Marcel: "On se retrouve demain à la piscine."

    b) Jules: "On se retrouve ce matin au centre-ville."

    c) Nadège: "On se retrouve lundi chez moi."

    d) Françoise: "On se retrouve au restaurant à vingt heures."

4 Use the words in the box to translate these sentences into French.

    a) Where shall we meet?

    b) How much does a ticket cost?

    c) I would like two tickets please.

    d) When shall we meet?

    e) A ticket costs three euros.

billet	billet	billets
Je On	On où	plaît
se se	s'il	trois
Un quand	Combien	
coûte	coûte	deux
retrouve	retrouve	euros
un	voudrais	vous

Practice Questions

5   Copy and complete these sentences to say how you get to various places.
The pictures show you what to say.   The first one has been done for you.

a)   Je vais à Dieppe _en bateau_

   b)   Je vais à la piscine ....

c)   Je vais au collège ....

   d)   Je vais au cinéma ....

e)   Je vais au centre-ville ....

   f)   Je vais au café ....

6   You're at a train station buying tickets. For each of the following, write out a
sentence in French to say what kind of ticket you want.   → = single, ⇆ = return.
The first one has been done for you.

a)   →   Toulouse 2nd.   *Je voudrais un aller simple pour*
                               Toulouse, en deuxième classe.

b)   ⇆   Paris 2nd.

c)   →   Nice 1st.

d)   →   Calais 2nd.

e)   ⇆   Marseille 1st.

⬭ **Track 14**   Listening Question

7   Copy out the timetable below, then listen to the CD and fill in the blanks.

Destination	Heure	Quai
Bordeaux	7.20	6
Dijon	8.45	
Le Mans	11.30	1
Nantes		4
Perpignan		2
Rouen	18.05	

Summary Questions

Section 5 is the most important section in my opinion — the A-Z guide to chatting people up and making social arrangements. Don't tell me you don't need to know this stuff.

1) What's the French for these sports?
   a) football b) table tennis c) cricket d) rugby e) tennis f) chess

2) In French, complete this sentence for each of the sports above: 'I play...'.

3) Write down the French for these instruments:
   a) trumpet b) guitar c) cello d) flute

4) In French, write out this sentence for each of the instruments above: 'I play...'.

5) What is the French for these activities?
   a) hiking b) skiing c) shopping d) cycling e) swimming f) ice skating

6) Pick from the sports, instruments and activities above, and complete these phrases, in French.
   a) I love.......   b) I like.......   c) I hate.......   d) Do you like......?

7) Marie-Claire watches television, she likes to listen to the radio, but she doesn't like to read books. How would she say that in French?

8) Jacques doesn't like to watch films. He likes to listen to music. He doesn't like to read newspapers. How would he say that in French?

9) Finish off this sentence in French, for each of the things listed below: 'I like...'
   a) this music b) this novel c) this magazine.

10) What do these sentences mean?
    a) Je n'aime pas ce film.   b) J'aime ce journal.

11) You meet your French friend in Kwik Save. Suggest going to these places:
    a) cinema b) town centre c) restaurant d) swimming pool

12) Write down three ways he could say 'yes' to your suggestions.

13) You meet Brigitte Bardot and she says these things to you. What do they mean?
    a) Allons au théâtre.   b) Allons au centre de loisirs.   c) Allons chez toi.

14) She looks a bit dodgy, so write down four ways you could say 'no'.

15) Write these out in French:
    a) Let's meet at ten o'clock. b) Let's meet tomorrow.
    c) Let's meet in front of the cinema.

16) Anne-Laure is at the cinema. She asks how much a ticket costs, and the kiosk-bloke says it costs four euros. Then she says she'd like two tickets please. Write their conversation out in French.

17) In French, complete this sentence for each of the types of transport: 'I go by...'
    a) train b) coach c) bus d) aeroplane e) underground f) car g) boat
    h) bicycle i) motorbike

18) Say 'I go on foot' out loud and in French.

19) How would you say this lot in French?
    'Is there a train to Calais? I would like a return, second class. What time does the train leave? What time does the train arrive? Which platform does the train leave from?'

SECTION FIVE — FREE TIME, HOBBIES AND TRANSPORT

Post Office

Shut down your e-mail and unplug that fax. It's back to the 60s — just <u>letters</u> and <u>phones</u>.

At the post office — À la poste

You can't send a <u>letter</u> without buying a <u>stamp</u> — so let's learn about stamps.

stamp: le timbre

a one-euro stamp: un timbre à un euro

a two-euro stamp: un timbre à deux euros

This is how you <u>ask</u> for a <u>stamp</u>:

For more on euros, see p.69.

Je voudrais un timbre à deux euros. = I'd like a two-euro stamp.

You'll have to ask how much if you want to <u>send a letter home</u>:

Je voudrais envoyer une lettre en Angleterre.

= I'd like to send a letter to England.

C'est combien? = How much is that?

Change 'Angleterre' to whatever country you need, e.g. Écosse. See p.105 for countries.

Some other post-related words

Here are the rest of the <u>posty words</u> you need to know:

letter: la lettre

postbox: la boîte aux lettres

postcard: la carte postale

address: l'adresse (f)

Just e-mail instead — much easier

You'll only need this stuff if you're the nice sort of person who writes postcards for friends when you're on holiday. If you're mean and lazy you can ignore this section on letters altogether.

Telephones

Phones — great invention. And they even work the same in France as at home. Wow.

Telephone numbers — Les numéros de téléphone

Learn this stuff for when you do a phone conversation,
or you listen to people talking about theirs.

telephone number:
le numéro de téléphone

You say your phone number in groups of 2
(e.g. twenty-eight, not two eight):

Mon numéro de téléphone est le vingt-huit, dix-neuf, cinquante-six.

= My telephone number is 28, 19, 56.

Phoning people in France

Here's what you say when you phone someone:

Allô — ici Dave.   = Hello, it's Dave here.

Je peux parler à Marie?   = Can I speak to Marie?

French people only say 'allô' when they're on the phone
If you said 'allô' to someone French normally, they'd know you were saying hello, but they'd
rather say 'bonjour' to you, until they phone you. Then they'd say 'allô'. Funny old world.

Informal Letters

You're more than likely to find yourself having to write a <u>letter</u> to a <u>penfriend</u>.
Pretty easy if you learn the <u>tricks</u> — you can even learn some <u>stock phrases</u> off by heart.

Start a letter with '**Cher Pierre**' — 'Dear Pierre'

Learn the <u>layout</u> of letters, and how to say 'Dear Somebody...', it's essential. This letter's short
on content, but it shows you how to <u>start</u> and <u>end</u> it properly, and where to put the <u>date</u>:

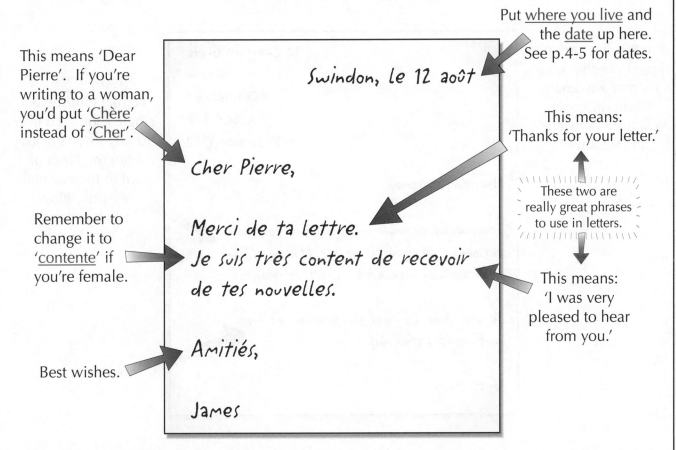

Put <u>where you live</u> and
the <u>date</u> up here.
See p.4-5 for dates.

This means 'Dear
Pierre'. If you're
writing to a woman,
you'd put '<u>Chère</u>'
instead of '<u>Cher</u>'.

This means:
'Thanks for your letter.'

These two are
really great phrases
to use in letters.

Remember to
change it to
'<u>contente</u>' if
you're female.

This means:
'I was very
pleased to hear
from you.'

Best wishes.

Swindon, le 12 août

Cher Pierre,

Merci de ta lettre.
Je suis très content de recevoir
de tes nouvelles.

Amitiés,

James

Don't panic if you have to write a <u>postcard</u> — just do the same as for a short letter.

Other **phrases** to use in your **letters**

Here's a useful phrase you can bung
in at the <u>start</u> of any informal letter.

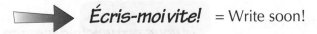 **Ça va?**   = How are you?

Stick this sentence in
<u>just before</u> you sign off.

Écris-moi vite!   = Write soon!

This is <u>another way</u> to sign off —
you can use it <u>instead of</u> 'amitiés'.

À bientôt.   = Bye for now.

Learn these phrases — you'll need them
Seven set phrases for you to learn. Don't forget that 'cher' changes to 'chère' if you're writing
to someone female, and 'content' changes to 'contente' if you're female yourself.

Formal Letters

You can't write to your bank manager the same way as you write to your mates. Formal letters need formal wording. The example on this page is booking a hotel room — see p.101 for more.

Learn the **special phrases** for **formal letters**

The trick with formal letters is all in the <u>starting</u> and the <u>ending</u>. Look at this beauty:

Put this if you <u>don't know</u> whether it's a man or a woman. If you <u>do</u> know, just put 'Monsieur' or 'Madame'.

10 Chestnut Grove
Piketon
Cheeseshire
GC4 2GP
le 10 janvier 1929

This lot means:
'I'd like to reserve a single room. I'd like to stay three nights, from the ninth of April to the eleventh of April. How much is that?'

Monsieur/Madame,

Je voudrais réserver une chambre pour une personne. Je voudrais rester trois nuits, du neuf avril au onze avril. C'est combien?

Je vous prie d'agréer l'expression de mes sentiments distingués,

Smita Jones

Yours sincerely.

This ending is <u>dead important</u>, so I've written it out <u>again</u> in big — <u>learn it</u> and churn it out: (just don't ask why it's so long)

Je vous prie d'agréer l'expression de mes sentiments distingués.

= Yours sincerely.

Another useful phrase to stick in:

Je vous remercie d'avance.

= Thank you in advance.

J — is that a formal letter?

Learn that phrase (the long, stupid one) really well. I guarantee it'll come in handy. You'll probably not need to write any formal letters to French bank managers just yet, but never mind.

Practice Questions

1. Here are some phrases from a post office. Write down what they mean in English.

   a) Je voudrais un timbre à trois euros.
   b) C'est combien?
   c) Je voudrais envoyer une lettre en France.
   d) Je voudrais deux timbres à quatre euros.

2. These are sentences from phone conversations. Copy and complete them by writing in the missing words. The bits in brackets are what they mean in English.

   a) **Magalie:** Allô — .... Magalie. *(Hello, it's Magalie here.)*

   b) **Laika:** Mon .... de .... est le dix-sept, cinquante, vingt-deux. *(My phone number is 17, 50, 22.)*

   c) **Magalie:** Je .... à James? *(Can I speak to James?)*

3. Write an informal letter, including all the information given below.

   • Write the letter to your friend Marie.　　• Ask her how she is.

   • Thank her for her letter.　　• Say that you're very pleased to hear from her.

   • Tell her to write to you soon.　　• Say "Bye for now" and add your name.

4. Read this letter and answer the questions.

   > *10 Meadow View*
   > *Herrington*
   > *Greathamp*
   > *GC3 2GP*
   >
   > *Madame, Monsieur,*
   >
   > *Je voudrais réserver une chambre pour une personne. Je voudrais rester cinq nuits, du dix janvier au quatorze janvier. C'est combien?*
   >
   > *Je vous prie d'agréer l'expression de mes sentiments distingués,*
   >
   > *George Smith*

   a) What kind of a place is George writing to?

   b) What sort of room does he want?

   c) How long is George going to stay?

   d) In which month does he want to go?

   e) What does he want to know?

Summary Questions

Short this section may be, but it's important. The only way to make sure you know it all is to do all these questions. If you get any wrong, go back and relearn it, then try the questions again. ...And cover up the pages when you're doing them, or it's just plain cheating.

1)   You're at a French post office. Ask for a one-euro stamp.

2)   Then say you want to send a letter to Scotland.

3)   Now ask for a two-euro stamp and say you want to send a letter to England.

4)   Say you want to send a postcard to Spain.

5)   Write these down in French:
    a)   stamp
    b)   letter
    c)   postbox
    d)   postcard
    e)   address

6)   Say what your own phone number is in French.

7)   Say these phone numbers in French:
    a)   236804
    b)   762494
    c)   189348
    d)   625730

8)   You're phoning your French friend, Jean-Paul. Say hello to the person who answers the phone, say who you are, and ask to speak to Jean-Paul.

9)   Write a letter to your female penfriend, Françoise. Ask her how she is, thank her for her letter, say you were pleased to hear from her, and say 'bye for now'.

10) What do the following phrases mean in English?
    a)   Ça va?
    b)   Écris-moi vite!
    c)   À bientôt.
    d)   Amitiés.

11) How do you start a formal letter in French?

12) How do you say these in French?
    a) Yours sincerely.
    b) Thank you in advance.

Weather

Weather — it's what we Brits like to talk about the most. Not sure about the French though...

Say what the weather's like — "Il fait ..."

This is the <u>question</u> you'll get asked about the weather:

Quel temps fait-il?   = What's the weather like?

A lot of the main types of weather start "<u>il fait</u>".

it's nice weather:
il fait beau

it's bad weather:
il fait mauvais

it's hot:
il fait chaud

it's cold:
il fait froid

it's windy:
il fait du vent

Say what the weather's like **without** saying "il fait"

1) <u>Raining</u>, and <u>snowing</u> are <u>different</u>. There's <u>no</u> "fait" in the sentence.

it's raining:
il pleut

it's snowing:
il neige

2) These weather types use "<u>il y a</u>" instead.

it's sunny:
il y a du soleil

it's cloudy:
il y a des nuages

it's foggy:
il y a du brouillard

it's stormy:
il y a de l'orage

Talk about the weather... go on, you know you want to

There are eleven weather phrases on this page... Learn them all off by heart as soon as you can.
Britain used to hold the Olympic record for talking about the weather. Make your country proud.

Seasons

You never know when you'll need to tell people, in French, about winter and summer.

The seasons — **Les saisons**

The seasons are dead useful. And there are only <u>four</u> of them to learn.

spring:
le printemps

summer:
l'été (m)

autumn:
l'automne (m)

winter:
l'hiver (m)

Talk about **what** you do **when**

The thing you're most likely to want to say about the <u>seasons</u> is what you <u>do</u> in which season. For example:

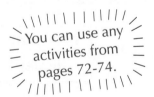

You can use any activities from pages 72-74.

En hiver, je fais du ski. = In winter, I go skiing.

in spring: au printemps
in summer: en été
in autumn: en automne

go shopping: fais du shopping
go hiking: fais des randonnées
watch the TV: regarde la télévision

In winter, spring, autumn and summer I just work... ho hum...

Don't forget about all those hobbies and activities on pages 72-74. It's really nice to be able to tie different phrases that you've learned together. So get going — remember those phrases.

Holidays

You need to talk about your own holidays, and understand other people talking about theirs.

Talk about where you normally go on **holiday**

The green bits are the questions you could get asked about holidays.
The blue bits are your answers — change the underlined bits to match your own holiday.

Où vas-tu en vacances d'habitude?

= Where do you go on holiday normally?

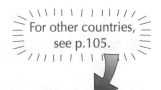
For other countries,
see p.105.

D'habitude, je vais en France.

= Normally, I go to France.

Avec qui vas-tu en vacances?

= Who do you go on holiday with?

For other people,
see p.19.

J'y vais avec mon père et ma sœur.

= I go there with my father and my sister.

Tu y vas pour combien de temps?

= For how long do you go there?

For other times,
see p.4.

J'y vais pour une semaine.

= I go there for one week.

No time for a holiday just yet... there's French to be learned

Cover half the page so you can only see the questions, then scribble down your answers.
Then look back at the page — if you got any wrong, do it again. A foolproof way to learn it.

Holidays

That's not all on holidays... Here's a whole other page of holiday questions and answers.

Some more questions about your **holidays**

Once again, the green bits are the questions you could get asked about holidays, and the blue bits are your answers — change the underlined bits to match your own holiday.

Où restes-tu d'habitude?

= Where do you normally stay?

Je reste dans un camping.

= I stay on a campsite.

For other places to stay, see p.99.

Qu'est-ce que tu fais?

= What do you do?

Je vais à la plage.

= I go to the beach.

For other things to do, see pages 72-74.

Quel temps fait-il d'habitude?

= What's the weather like normally?

Il fait du soleil.

= It's sunny.

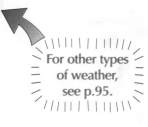

For other types of weather, see p.95.

Get yourself down to the beach... you've earned it

Well done. If you've worked your way through all this lot, you've done well. You deserve a holiday. But it's not over until it stays in your head for good, so read over it a few more times.

Hotels and Camping

All the words you need to know about hotels, hostels and camping, all on one page. Great.

Learn these **places to stay**

These are the <u>absolute basics</u> for talking about places to stay.
You <u>have</u> to know these — or you'll end up booking your tent into a hotel or something...

hotel:
l'hôtel (m)

campsite:
le camping

youth hostel:
l'auberge de jeunesse (f)

At the campsite — **Au camping**

You'll need these for talking about things around the <u>campsite</u> — whether you're into the <u>outdoor life</u> or not.

tent:
une tente

caravan:
une caravane

pitch (space for a tent):
un emplacement

sleeping bag:
un sac de couchage

drinking water:
l'eau potable (f)

Camping — fresh air, cold beans, and ants...

There's nothing to worry yourself about here — it's all fairly straightforward. Some words are even really easy to learn — 'une tente', for example, isn't going to cause you any nightmares.

At the Hotel

It's not over yet... There's a few more things to learn before you can stay at any French hotels.

At the hotel — À l'hôtel

Just to give you more to learn, hotels have <u>different kinds of rooms</u>. Here they are:

| room: une chambre | room for one person: une chambre pour une personne | room for two people: une chambre pour deux personnes |

Here's how to describe <u>hotel rooms</u> in a little more detail.
This'll come in handy for <u>booking</u> them (on the next page).

une chambre avec douche = a room with a shower

single room: chambre individuelle
double room: chambre double

bath: bain
balcony: balcon
bathroom: salle de bains
toilets: toilettes

Some more **hotel** related words to learn

| dining room: la salle à manger | key: la clé | telephone: le téléphone | toilets: les toilettes |

Learn this well... you'll need it again
You'll need this stuff again when it comes to the 'booking accommodation' bit of the book.
So make sure you know all these pieces of vocab really well, and the rest will be easy.

Booking Accommodation

Checking into a hotel, or writing to book a room, are typical role play or writing test stuff. Plus this stuff is useful for actually having a holiday in France. Bonus.

Booking a **hotel room** — tell them **what** and **when**

Booking a room isn't hard if you learn this stuff. Take these phrases, and <u>tweak</u> them for the <u>number of nights</u> / <u>dates</u> you want. The <u>questions</u> you'll be asked are in <u>blue</u>.

① *Avez-vous des chambres libres?*   = Have you any rooms free?

C'est pour combien de personnes?   = For how many people?

② *Je voudrais une chambre individuelle.*   = I would like a single room.

> *a double room:*
> une chambre double

C'est pour combien de nuits?   = For how many nights?

③ *Je voudrais rester une nuit.*   = I would like to stay for one night.

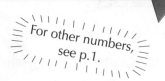
For other numbers, see p.1.

> *two nights:* deux nuits
> *one week:* une semaine
> *two weeks:* deux semaines

C'est pour quelle date?   = What date's it for?

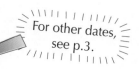
For other dates, see p.3.

④ *Je voudrais rester du onze août au douze août.*

= I would like to stay from the eleventh of August to the twelfth of August.

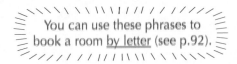
You can use these phrases to book a room <u>by letter</u> (see p.92).

⑤ *C'est combien?*   = How much is that?

This is hard stuff... but you can do it

Read through the page, then cover it up and write down what you'd say to book a <u>single room</u>, for <u>one week</u>, from the <u>1st of April</u> to the <u>7th of April</u>. Then check it against the page.

Booking Accommodation

Obviously, you might not be able to afford €100 a night for a hotel in France... so you should learn how to stay at much more affordable campsites instead.

Booking into a **campsite** — **don't** ask for a **room**

You use the <u>exact same</u> phrases to book into a <u>campsite</u> as for booking into a hotel — except the <u>first two</u> (you don't get <u>rooms</u> in a campsite).

① *Avez-vous des emplacements libres?* = Have you any pitches free?

② *Je voudrais un emplacement pour une tente.*

= I would like a pitch for a tent.

> *a caravan:* une caravane

Some more phrases for the **campsite**

Où sont les toilettes? = Where are the toilets?

> *the showers:* les douches
> *the bins:* les poubelles

Est-ce qu'il y a un magasin? = Is there a shop?

> *a swimming pool:* une piscine

So don't go to a campsite and ask for a room
More practice — pretend you're booking into a campsite. Ask if they have any pitches free, then ask for a pitch for a tent. Say you're staying for three nights, then ask how much it is.

Practice Questions

Track 15

<u>Listening Question</u>

1   Listen to Marie describing the weather in her home town, then answer the
    questions below.

    a)   When is it cold?
    b)   Why does Marie like winter?
    c)   What is the weather like in autumn?
    d)   In which two seasons does Marie say it rains?
    e)   What is the weather like in summer?

2   This is a weather map of France. Write down, in
    French, what the weather is like at these places.

    a)   Strasbourg   b)   Marseille

    c)   Le Havre   d)   Bordeaux

    e)   Lyon   f)   Paris

3   Read what François has written about his
    holiday, then answer the questions below.

    a)   Where does he normally go?

    b)   Who does he go with?

    c)   How long do they go for?

    d)   Where do they stay?

    e)   What does he do when it rains?

    f)   When does he go to the beach?

D'habitude, je vais en Espagne.
J'y vais avec mon père, ma mère et le chien.
J'y vais pour dix jours et je reste dans un hôtel.
Quand il fait du soleil, je vais à la plage,
mais quand il pleut, je regarde la télévision.

4   Describe the holidays below in French. We've given you some of the words
    you'll need.

    a)   I go to Italy with my Mum for three weeks. (Italy = Italie)

    b)   I go to Germany for a week. I stay on a campsite. (Germany = Allemagne)

    c)   I go to France and go to the beach.

    d)   I go to Scotland. It's sunny.

Practice Questions

5   Pierre is lost in England — read his questions below and write down the
English for the things he's asking for.

a)   Où est l'auberge de jeunesse?   b)   Où est le téléphone?

c)   Où est la salle à manger?   d)   Où est l'hôtel?

e)   Où sont les toilettes?   f)   Où est ma clé?

g)   Où est la salle de bains?   h)   Où est le camping?

6   Write down in French how you would describe the rooms below.

a) 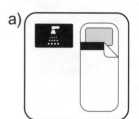   b) 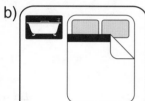   c) 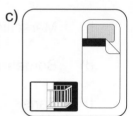   d)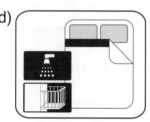

(**Track 16**)   <u>Listening Question</u>

7   Listen to this conversation at a hotel reception, then write down if the statements
below are true or false.

a)   They want a double room with a bathroom.
b)   They only want one room.
c)   They want to stay for 5 nights.
d)   The total bill is 800 euros.
e)   Breakfast is not included.

---

8   You're trying to book into a campsite in France. Copy and complete the
following conversation by translating the English in brackets into French.

Vous: *[Have you any pitches free?]*

Réceptionniste: Peut-être. C'est pour une tente ou une caravane?

Vous: *[I would like a pitch for a tent please.]*

Réceptionniste: C'est pour combien de nuits?

Vous: *[I would like to stay for four nights. How much is that?]*

Réceptionniste: € 30.

Countries

Glory be, it's a great big map...
Don't get carried away by the pretty colours — look at the country names and learn them.

The countries of Europe — **Les pays d'Europe**

"le pays" = country

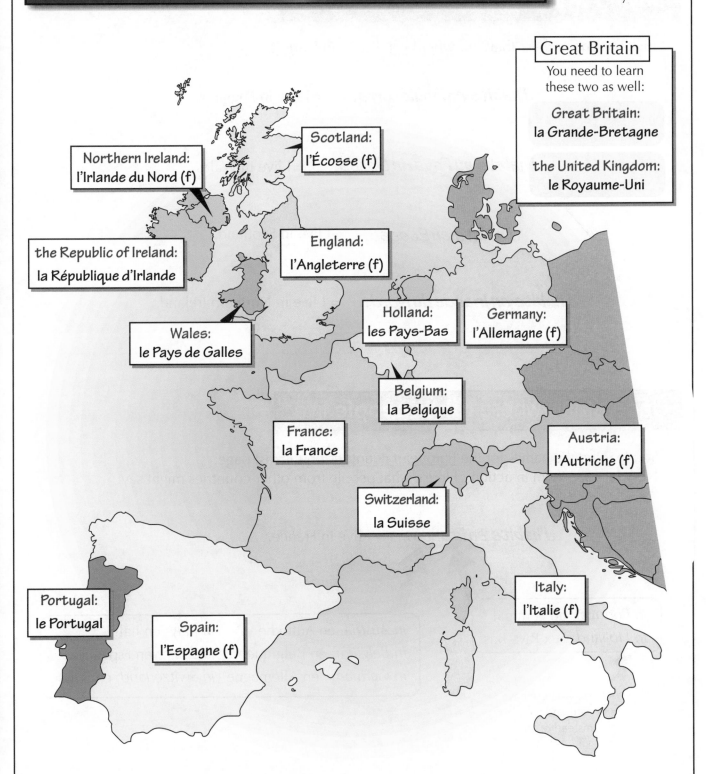

Great Britain

You need to learn these two as well:

Great Britain: **la Grande-Bretagne**

the United Kingdom: **le Royaume-Uni**

Scotland: l'Écosse (f)

Northern Ireland: l'Irlande du Nord (f)

the Republic of Ireland: la République d'Irlande

England: l'Angleterre (f)

Holland: les Pays-Bas

Germany: l'Allemagne (f)

Wales: le Pays de Galles

Belgium: la Belgique

France: la France

Austria: l'Autriche (f)

Switzerland: la Suisse

Portugal: le Portugal

Spain: l'Espagne (f)

Italy: l'Italie (f)

Learn your countries — they come up loads in exams

There are <u>16</u> countries to learn. You should be able write down <u>all 16 of them</u> from memory.
Close the book and give it a go. Lucky for you, some of them are <u>easy</u> — like <u>la France</u>.

SECTION SEVEN — WEATHER, HOLIDAYS AND COUNTRIES

Nationalities

You'll get asked about where you're from. And if you've learnt this, you'll be able to answer. Simple as that. ...With the added bonus that nobody'll think you're Dutch by mistake.

Saying where you live — J'habite...

Pick the one of these that's for where you live, and learn it.

J'habite en Angleterre.   = I live in England.

J'habite au Pays de Galles.   = I live in Wales.

J'habite en Écosse.   = I live in Scotland.

J'habite en Irlande du Nord.   = I live in Northern Ireland.

Understand where other people live

You learned the names for the European countries on the last page.
Now let's see them in action. Here's what people from other countries might say:

J'habite en France.   = I live in France.

in Portugal: au Portugal
in Holland: aux Pays-Bas

Look — these have
'au' and 'aux'
instead of 'en'.

in Austria: en Autriche	*in Italy:* en Italie
in Belgium: en Belgique	*in Spain:* en Espagne
in Germany: en Allemagne	*in Switzerland:* en Suisse

Of course, you might live in Spain yourself, in which case — ¡hola!
Keep practising these. Just say where you live a few times (in French, obviously), then pretend you're from some other countries and do the same. (Do the funny accent or it's not the same.)

Nationalities

Here's a little variation on the theme. Instead of saying 'I am from England / Scotland / Wales / Northern Ireland', you can say 'I am English / Scottish / Welsh / Northern Irish'. Handy.

Saying your nationality — **Je suis...**

This is how you put the sentence together:

> **'Je suis'** + NATIONALITY

Je suis britannique.

= I am British.

Learn all these **nationalities**

Here are some common ones to get you started. Learn them well:

Je suis écossais(e) .   = I am Scottish.

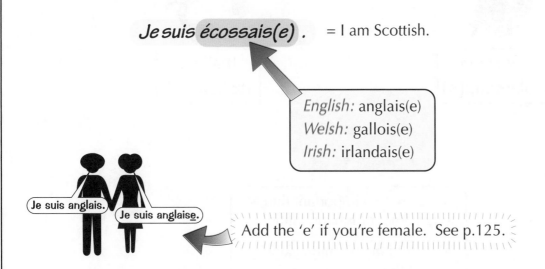

English: anglais(e)
Welsh: gallois(e)
Irish: irlandais(e)

Je suis anglais.
Je suis anglaise.

Add the 'e' if you're female. See p.125.

Important bit:
Don't use a capital letter
for anglais, écossais etc.

Don't forget to add an 'e' if you're a girl

...otherwise you're pretty much telling people that you're a boy. Of course, if you are a boy, don't add an 'e' by mistake, or you'll be telling people that you're a girl. Got that? Good.

Nationalities

It's all very well being able to understand people telling you that they're English, but it's more likely that people speaking French will be telling you they're from somewhere outside the UK.

Learn these **European nationalities**

Learn these four <u>nationalities</u> as well, so you can understand where people from different places in Europe come from.

French:
français(e)

Spanish:
espagnol(e)

German:
allemand(e)

Italian:
italien(ne)

There are two important things to remember for nationalities:

- Add the bit in <u>brackets</u> if the person is <u>female</u>.
- <u>Don't</u> use a <u>capital letter</u>.

Je suis italienne, so tell me why I'm speaking French...?

I'll tell you a secret — the words for the <u>languages</u> are the same as the <u>nationalities</u>. So a <u>person</u> can be 'français', and the <u>language</u> they speak is 'français' as well. Check out p.38 on school subjects.

Practice Questions

1   Here's a list of the countries in the UK. Write down their names in French.

    a)   England   b)   Wales

    c)   Scotland   d)   Northern Ireland

2   Here's a list of some European countries written in French.
Write down their names in English.

    a) les Pays-Bas   b) l'Allemagne   c) la Belgique

    d) la France   e) le Royaume-Uni   f) l'Autriche

    g) la Suisse   h) l'Italie   i) l'Espagne

    j) le Portugal   k) la Grande-Bretagne

3   Imagine that you are each of these people. Write down how they would
describe their nationality in French. The first one has been done for you.

    a) Navpreet   *Je suis irlandaise.*

    b) Ruth

    c) Brian

    d) James

HINT: Watch out for whether it should be masculine or feminine.

Track 17   Listening Question

4   Listen to Pierre describing the people on his campsite, then answer the
questions below.

    a) Where does Pierre live?
    b) Which two people are from Spain?
    c) Where does Francesca come from?
    d) What nationality is Gerhard?
    e) What nationality is Gerry?
    f) Where does Gerry live?
    g) Where does Lisa come from?

Summary Questions

Here's fourteen questions about all the stuff in Section 7 — use these to check what you know, and what you need to learn. Work through all the questions and check which ones you couldn't do. Then go back through the section to find out the answers, leave it a few minutes, and redo the questions. Keep at it till you can do them all.

1) Your French friend, Françoise, wants to know what the weather is like where you are. Say that it's sunny, hot and windy.

2) Now ask Françoise what the weather's like with her (in French, obviously).

3) Françoise says it's cold and raining. How would she say that in French?

4) She says 'il fait mauvais'. What does that mean in English?

5) How do you say the following in French?
a) it's cloudy   b) it's stormy   c) it's foggy

6) What's the French for:
a) winter   b) spring   c) autumn   d) summer

7) Your friend Pierre asks what you normally do in the winter.
Tell him that in the winter, you go skiing.

8) While you're at it, tell him that in the summer you go hiking and in the autumn you just watch TV.

9) Pierre wants to know all about your holidays. Tell him this in French:
Normally I go to Spain. I go with my brother.
I go for two weeks. I stay in a youth hostel. I go walking.

10) You've changed your mind about your holidays. Tell Pierre this instead:
Normally I go to France. I go with my mother and sister.
I go for one week. I stay in a hotel. I go to the beach. It's sunny.

11) What are these in French?
a) hotel   b) youth hostel   c) campsite

12) How do you say these in French?
a) drinking water   b) sleeping bag   c) pitch   d) caravan   e) tent

13) How do you say these in French?
a) key   b) single room   c) dining room   d) room with a balcony
e) double room   f) double room with a bath

14) You arrive at a swanky hotel in France. Ask them if they have any rooms free.

15) Say you want a double room for five nights. Ask how much it costs.

16) You arrive at a campsite. Ask if there are any pitches free.

17) Say you want a pitch for a caravan and want to stay from 8th June to 19th June.

18) Ask where the showers are and if there's a shop.

19) Write down the four countries in the UK and five other countries, in French.

20) Say which country you live in (yep, in French).

21) Write down the nationality (in French) to go with each of these places:
a) France   b) Wales   c) Italy   d) England   e) Scotland   f) Germany
g) Ireland   h) Spain

Opinions

Try and get into the habit of <u>saying what you think</u> and giving your <u>opinion</u>.

Talk about your likes...

You'll often need to say what you <u>like</u>. Here are a couple of ways of saying it:

J'aime = I like

J'aime le chocolat. = I like chocolate.

J'adore = I love

J'adore les bananes = I love bananas.

and your dislikes...

Je n'aime pas = I don't like

Je n'aime pas le tennis. = I don't like tennis.

Je déteste = I hate

Je déteste le chou-fleur = I hate cauliflower.

Don't keep your opinions to yourself

Just one piece of advice: If you want to say 'I love you', don't say "J'adore tu" — that's wrong for so many reasons. The French for 'I love you' is actually "Je t'aime". See page 123 for why.

Opinions

Once you've said you like or dislike something, you'd better back it up with a good <u>reason</u>.

Explain yourself

When you're explaining <u>why</u> you like or hate something, use this handy phrase:

PARCE QUE + C'EST + DESCRIBING WORD

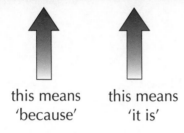

this means
'because'

this means
'it is'

Examples

Have a look at these <u>examples</u>, then make up some sentences of your own.

J'aime la chimie parce que c'est intéressant.

= I like chemistry because it's interesting.

Je n'aime pas les maths parce que c'est difficile.

= I don't like maths because it's difficult.

J'adore jouer au football parce que c'est amusant.

= I love playing football because it's fun.

It doesn't matter what you say, just give a good reason
I like chocolate because it's delicious, I hate clowns because they're scary. Whatever. Don't worry about what you're saying — say anything at all, just make sure you say it in French.

Asking Questions

You won't get very far in life if you don't ask any <u>questions</u>. These are the key <u>question words</u>.

Where? — Où?

Où habites-tu? = Where do you live?

Who? — Qui?

Qui est là? = Who's there?

When? — Quand?

Quand est ton anniversaire? = When is your birthday?

Which / what? — Quel(le)?

Quelle est ta matière préférée? = What's your favourite subject?

How much? — Combien?

Combien coûte ce pull? = How much is this jumper?

Any more questions? Anyone?

You'll probably know all these already. I expect that in your first ever French lesson, you were asked who you were, how old you were and where you lived. So you should be used to it...

Asking Questions

You can use these two magic expressions to turn statements into questions. Read on.

'Est-ce que' makes a statement into a question

You don't really need to worry about what the different bits of 'est-ce que' mean.
You just need to know how to use it:

1) Start with a simple sentence.

> **Elle a un frère.**   = She has a brother.

2) Stick 'est-ce que' at the beginning, and it turns into a question.

> **Est-ce qu'elle a un frère?**   = Does she have a brother?

When the next word starts with a vowel, you put an apostrophe instead of the 'e' of 'que'.

Use 'Qu'est-ce que' for questions starting with 'What...?'

This is almost the same as the one above, but you need to use it to make questions that start with 'What'...

> **Qu'est-ce que c'est?**   = What's that?

> **Qu'est-ce que tu fais le week-end?**   = What do you do at the weekend?

Est-ce que c'est une question?
The other really important thing is that you have to make your voice go up at the end when you're asking a question in French. It's the French way. Practise in the bath or something.

Words for People and Objects

<u>Nouns</u> are words for <u>people</u> and <u>objects</u>. Every French noun is either <u>masculine</u> or <u>feminine</u>. Don't ask me why.

French nouns are either **masculine** or **feminine**

Yep, it's not as simple as just learning the French word for things — you also need to learn if they're <u>masculine</u> or <u>feminine</u>.

> ### The Golden Rule
> Each time you learn a word, remember the 'le' or 'la' to go with it — don't think 'dog = chien', think 'dog = le chien'.

Le chien.

You need different words for 'a' and 'the'

Masculine and feminine words need different words for 'the' and 'a'.

Masculine

the pen: **le stylo** (masculine)

a pen: **un stylo** (masculine)

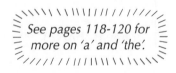

See pages 118-120 for more on 'a' and 'the'.

Feminine

the ruler: **la règle** (feminine)

a ruler: **une règle** (feminine)

Why can't nouns all be the same gender?
There's just no easy answer to this one, sadly. They're not, and that's that. Of course, it'd be a lot easier if you were born in France and you'd just learnt it all naturally as a baby, but hey...

Making Nouns Plural

Now you've learnt about French <u>nouns</u>, you'll want to know how to use them when there's <u>more than one</u>.

A **plural** is **more than one** of something

It's simple, really. <u>Bananas</u> is the plural of <u>banana</u>. You probably already knew that. You usually make a plural just by adding '<u>s</u>', like you do in English.

| *le chat* | = the cat |
| *les chats* | = the cats |

Les chats.

Each time you learn a word, learn how to make it into a plural too.

There are some **exceptions** to the rule

It's funny how every rule has some exceptions, just to make things a bit trickier. All you have to do is learn these common exceptions, and you'll be fine.

oeil (eye)	**yeux (eyes)**
animal (animal)	**animaux (animals)**
cheval (horse)	**chevaux (horses)**
bateau (boat)	**bateaux (boats)**

For words that end in "eau" you generally add an "x" on the end for the plural.

Funny how plural is actually singular... (plurals is plural)
I suppose you could just never talk about animals, eyes, boats or horses in French. But that could be very awkward if they do come up in conversation, so you'd better learn these plurals.

Practice Questions

1   Copy and complete these French sentences. The bits in brackets tell you what to say.

    a)   Je n'aime pas le football .... [because it's boring]

    b)   J'aime la chimie .... [because it's useful]

    c)   J'adore regarder la télévision .... [because it's interesting]

    d)   Je déteste le collège .... [because it's difficult]

2   Write out these questions in English.

    a)   Quel âge as-tu?

    b)   Combien coûte ce livre?

    c)   Où habites-tu?

    d)   Quand est ton anniversaire?

    e)   Qui est cette fille?

    f)   Où est le théâtre?

3   Write out these sentences, changing 'un' or 'une' to 'deux', and changing the underlined nouns into plurals.

    a)   J'ai un <u>chat</u>.

    b)   Il aime une <u>fille</u>.

    c)   Pierre mange un <u>gâteau</u>.

    d)   Claire a un <u>frère</u>.

    e)   Il a un <u>animal</u>.

How to Say 'The'

You've already covered this a bit on pages 115-116, but here's <u>exactly</u> how to say 'the' in French.

The — **le, la**

In French, you use a different word for 'the', depending on whether the word's <u>masculine</u>, <u>feminine</u> or <u>plural</u> (see pages 115-116).

le garçon   = the boy

Words that mean 'the' are called definite articles.

la fille   = the girl

If the word starts with a vowel, use **l'**

If the word starts with <u>a</u>, <u>e</u>, <u>i</u>, <u>o</u>, <u>u</u>, the '<u>le</u>' or '<u>la</u>' is shortened to <u>l'</u>. This is also true for some words starting with '<u>h</u>'.

L'orange.

l'orange   = the orange

l'hôpital   = the hospital

Always use '**les**' for a plural

Look back at p. 116 for <u>more</u> on this.

les oranges   = the oranges

les garçons   = the boys

Learn these rules

If you learn the ways of saying 'the', you'll be off to a really good start with French grammar. It does get a teeny bit more complicated later on, but you'll cope with it, no problem.

How to Say 'To the' and 'At the'

You don't just need to say '<u>the</u>' when you're speaking French — you'll need some other things like '<u>to the</u>' and '<u>at the</u>' if you want to get by.

Add **à** to make 'to the' and 'at the'

The words '<u>le</u>' and '<u>les</u>' change when you put them after the word '<u>à</u>'. That's just because you <u>can't</u> say '<u>à le</u>' or '<u>à les</u>'. This handy chart shows you how to do it:

	le	la	l'	les
+ à	au	à la	à l'	aux

la and l' don't change

Je vais à	**+**	la piscine	**=**	Je vais <u>à la</u> piscine
				= I go to the swimming pool.

Je vais à	**+**	le café	**=**	Je vais <u>au</u> café
				= I go to the café.

Jouer à — to play something

You also have to use 'à' with some <u>verbs</u>. The one you're most likely to use is '<u>jouer à</u>'.

Je joue à	**+**	le tennis	**=**	Je joue <u>au</u> tennis
				= I play tennis.

Je joue à	**+**	les échecs	**=**	Je joue <u>aux</u> échecs
				= I play chess.

This isn't too bad once you get used to it
When you start seeing tables of grammar to learn, it always looks a little bit scary. The thing is, it's pretty simple as long as you know if the noun's masculine or feminine. Just practise it.

How to Say 'A'

You probably take the word '<u>a</u>' for granted in English. Here's how to say it in French.

'A' — un, une

In English, it's <u>easy</u> — you just use 'a' for any word (<u>a girl</u>, <u>a boy</u>, whatever).

In French, you need to know whether the word is <u>masculine</u> or <u>feminine</u>: it's <u>un</u> for <u>masculine</u> words, <u>une</u> for <u>feminine</u> words.

masculine	feminine
un	*une*

Grammar fans — these are called indefinite articles.

Un and une in action

J'ai <u>un</u> frère.   = I have a brother.

J'ai <u>une</u> soeur.   = I have a sister.

J'ai un frère.

J'ai une sœur.

Don't read this page indefinitely

OK, that's a pretty appalling pun, but at least if you understood it it proves you know that 'un' and 'une' are indefinite articles. Hang in there, there's more grammar to come.

'Some' and 'Any'

There are <u>four ways</u> of saying '<u>some</u>' or '<u>any</u>' in French.

Learn these four little words

How you say 'some' or 'any' depends on whether the word is masculine, feminine or plural, and whether it starts with a vowel or not.

	masculine singular	feminine singular	in front of a vowel	masculine or feminine plural
	le (or un)	*la* (or une)	*l'*	*les*
+ de	*du*	*de la*	*de l'*	*des*

Examples

Have a look at these examples, then try and make up some sentences of your own.

de + le = du   ***Avez-vous du pain?***   = Have you got any bread?

de + la = de la   ***Elle mange de la glace.***   = She eats some ice-cream.

de + l' = de l'   ***Il boit de l'Orangina.***   = He's drinking some Orangina.

de + les = des   ***J'ai des pommes.***   = I have some apples.

Some grammar to learn here
These are called partitive articles, by the way. But you don't need to learn that. You really do need to learn how to say 'some' and 'any'. It comes up all the time.

SECTION EIGHT — GRAMMAR AND PHRASES

I, You, He, She

These types of words are called pronouns. They're words that replace nouns, like 'you', 'she' or 'them'.

Learn these subject pronouns

These are the ones you'll use most often. They're the pronouns for 'I', 'you', 'he', etc.

je	I
tu	you (informal singular)
il	he/it
elle	she/it
on	one
nous	we
vous	you (formal singular, or plural)
ils	they (masculine, or mixed masculine/feminine)
elles	they (feminine)

They're for when the word you're replacing is the main person / thing in a sentence that's doing the action ('the subject'):

Le garçon lit le livre. = The boy reads the book.

Il lit le livre. = He reads the book.

Pronouns are surprisingly useful really

Just think what life would be like without pronouns. If you wanted to tell someone that you went to the zoo, you'd have to say 'Billy went to the zoo', and then you'd sound like an idiot.

Me, You, Him, Her

Remember me telling you that 'I love you' is 'Je t'aime'? Well now you get to find out what that little 't' in the middle is for. It's a direct object pronoun, that's what it is.

Me, te, le, la are direct object pronouns

These are direct object pronouns. They're for when the word you're replacing is the person / thing in a sentence that's having the action done to it (the 'direct object'). In English, you'd say 'me', 'she', 'it', 'them', etc. You need to learn the French words for them as well.

me	me
te	you (informal singular)
le	him / it
la	her / it
nous	us
vous	you (formal singular, or plural)
les	them

Here are some **examples**

1) Look at this example in English:

subject direct object   subject   direct object
                                              pronoun

2) It works the same way in French, but the direct object comes <u>before</u> the verb:

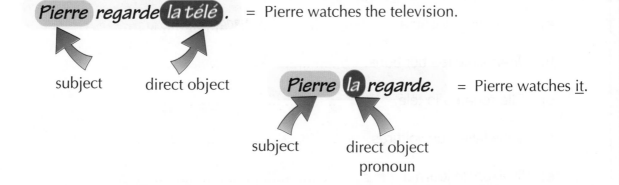

Pierre regarde la télé. = Pierre watches the television.

subject direct object

Pierre la regarde. = Pierre watches <u>it</u>.

subject direct object
         pronoun

I like it = I it like = Je l'aime... or something...

Don't worry if you don't get this at first — it's quite advanced stuff. Just learn what the direct object pronouns are for each person or group of people, then worry about the rest later.

Practice Questions

1 Copy out these sentences, then use one of the combinations from the box to fill in the gaps. Then write each sentence out in English. The feminine nouns are marked (f) and the masculine ones are marked (m). The first one has been done for you.

au	à la	à l'	aux

a) Je vais ....*à l'*.... école. (f) ....*I go to school.*........................

b) Je vais .... piscine. (f) ....

c) Je joue .... football. (m) ....

d) Ils jouent .... échecs (m, pl) ....

e) Nous allons .... cinéma (m) ....

2 Copy out the words below, and add 'un' or 'une' to say 'a', depending on whether they're masculine or feminine.

a) .... règle   b) .... cahier   c) .... classe

d) .... pomme   e) .... lapin   f) .... télévision

g) .... garçon   h) .... chambre   i) .... sac

3 Write out the sentences below, replacing the underlined words (direct objects) with one of the direct object pronouns from the box. The first one has been done for you.

le	la	les

a) Je mange le gâteau.   ....*Je le mange.*...................

b) Jean aime les bonbons.   ....

c) Elle regarde la télé.   ....

d) Vous lavez les voitures.   ....

e) Ils lisent le journal.   ....

f) Tu bois le café.   ....

Words to Describe Things

Describing words (<u>adjectives</u>) help you make your French sound interesting. If you don't use them, you'll sound <u>incredibly dull</u>.

Adjectives 'agree' with the thing they're describing

1) In <u>English</u>, describing words ('adjectives') stay the <u>same</u> whatever they're describing — e.g. a small boy, a small girl, small children, a small dog, a small house.

2) In <u>French</u>, adjectives have to <u>change</u> depending on the word they're describing — whether it's <u>masculine</u> or <u>feminine</u>, and <u>singular</u> or <u>plural</u>.

Learn these **two rules**

1) Add an '<u>s</u>' to the describing word if the word being described is <u>plural</u> (see p. 116).

le grand garçon   ➡   *les grand<u>s</u> garçon<u>s</u>*

the <u>big</u> boy   the <u>big</u> boy<u>s</u>

2) Add an '<u>e</u>' to the describing word if the word being described is <u>feminine</u> (see p. 115). (Only do this if the describing word doesn't already end in 'e'.)

la grand<u>e</u> fille   ➡   *les grand<u>es</u> fille<u>s</u>*

the <u>big</u> girl   the <u>big</u> girl<u>s</u>

So for a feminine plural you have to add an 'e' and an 's'.

There are some **exceptions**

There are some words that <u>don't just</u> get an 'e' for the feminine.
You need to <u>learn</u> the common ones.

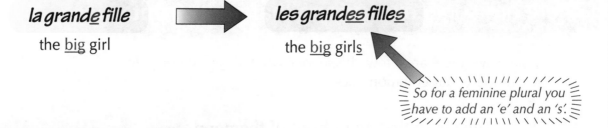

	m	**f**			**m**	**f**
white:	blanc	blanche	*kind:*		gentil	gentille
old:	vieux	vieille	*awful:*		affreux	affreuse
new:	neuf	neuve	*boring:*		ennuyeux	ennuyeuse
beautiful:	beau	belle				

Always make sure your adjectives agree

This is one of those golden rules that'll come in handy forever. Or at least as long as you're learning French. Always check your work to make sure that your adjectives agree.

Words to Describe Things

Using describing words (<u>adjectives</u>) isn't exactly the same as in English — you need to know <u>where</u> to put them in the sentence as well.

Most describing words go **after** the noun

1) In English, describing words always go <u>in front</u> of the word they're describing (e.g. you say '<u>black cat</u>' not '<u>cat black</u>'.

 2) It's different in French. Most describing words go <u>after</u> the word they're describing.

> *J'ai un chat <u>noir</u>.* = I have a <u>black</u> cat.
> (literally, 'I have a cat black.')

There are some **exceptions** that go **in front**

1) As always, there are a few cheeky ones that <u>always go in front</u>. Learn these four common ones:

Adjectives that go in front of the noun

big: grand(e)	*old:* vieux/vieille
small: petit(e)	*young:* jeune

> *J'ai un <u>petit</u> chien.* = I have a <u>small</u> dog.

Learn these four exceptions and you'll be fine
You do need to learn the adjectives that go in front of the nouns, because, typically, they're really common ones that come up all the time. Get used to the way they look in front.

Making Comparisons

Here's a useful trick — if you're trying to <u>describe</u> something and you can't think what to say, just <u>compare</u> it to something else.

'Plus' means more and 'moins' means less

In French, you can't say '<u>bigger</u>' or '<u>smaller</u>', you have to say '<u>more big</u>' or '<u>more small</u>'. Just add '<u>plus</u>' or '<u>moins</u>' in front of the adjective.

The word for '<u>more</u>' is <u>PLUS</u>.   Use <u>QUE</u> to say '<u>than</u>'.

Je suis plus grande que Sarah.   = I am taller than Sarah.

The word for '<u>less</u>' is <u>MOINS</u>.   Use <u>QUE</u> to say '<u>than</u>'.

Il est moins beau que Tom.   = He is less handsome than Tom.

Some words don't need 'plus'

As usual, there are a few <u>exceptions</u> to the rule. You can't say 'bigger' in French, but you can say '<u>better</u>' and '<u>worse</u>'. It's not tricky though, just learn which ones don't need 'plus'.

Je chante mieux que Fred.

Three comparisons that don't need 'PLUS'	
bien *(well)*	→ mieux *(better)*
mauvais *(bad)*	→ pire *(worse)*
bon *(good)*	→ meilleur *(better)*

= I sing better than Fred.

'Aussi' means as

To say '<u>as</u>' you need to use '<u>aussi</u>' in French. Use it in the same way as '<u>plus</u>' and '<u>moins</u>'.

Anne est aussi jeune que Julie.   = Anne is as young as Julie.

This page is better than the last page

See, you'll definitely need to use comparisons. You'll often hear people in listening practices going on about how they're taller than their brother, and other thrilling stuff like that.

Making Comparisons

Now you know how to say 'better' or 'worse' you'll need to know 'best' and 'worst' as well. These are called superlatives, by the way, but you don't need to remember that.

'Le / La plus' means 'the most'

On page 127, you found out that you can't say 'bigger' or 'smaller' in French. Well, you can't say 'biggest' or 'smallest' either. You need to use the words 'LE/LA PLUS' to say 'the most big' or 'the most small' instead.

It's LE PLUS here because Pierre is masculine.

Pierre est _le plus_ vieux.
 = Pierre is the oldest.
(literally 'Pierre is the most old.')

It's LA PLUS here because Hélène is feminine.

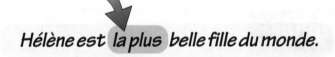

Hélène est _la plus_ belle fille du monde.
 = Hélène is the most beautiful girl in the world.

There are **three** exceptions to the rule

There are three odd ones out that you need to learn. These work just like in English — you don't need 'plus'.

bien (well)	➡	le/la mieux (the best)
bon (good)	➡	le/la meilleur(e) (the best)
mauvais (bad)	➡	le/la pire (worst)

Mon vélo est _le meilleur_. = My bike is the best.

Superlatives are useful for the Guinness Book of Records
I could have said that this page was the best, but it's a pretty rubbish joke. Superlatives are another example of why you need to know whether a noun is masculine or feminine.

'My' and 'Your'

This is the essential stuff — these words are used all the time. Just try speaking English without them and you'll see what I mean.

How to say 'my', 'your', 'our'...

1) In English, there's only one word each for 'my', 'your' etc. so it's pretty easy.

2) In French, the word you use changes to match the thing that it's describing — you have to choose masculine, feminine or plural.

Look at this example of how 'my' changes

Mon frère est grand, **ma soeur** est petite.

= My brother is big, my sister is small.

BUT before a word that starts with a vowel, you always use the masculine form.
This makes it easier to say:

Mon amie Anne est une fille.   = My friend Anne is a girl.

Learn this table

This table shows you all the different ways of saying 'my', 'your' etc.

	masculine singular	feminine singular	plural
MY	mon	ma	mes
YOUR	ton	ta	tes
HIS/HER/ITS	son	sa	ses
OUR	notre	notre	nos
YOUR	votre	votre	vos
THEIR	leur	leur	leurs

The plural ones all end in 's' by the way
That's a handy tip that reminds you they're plural. You just have to learn the table though, I'm afraid. Once you've seen a few in French reading comprehensions, they don't look so hard.

'This' and 'These'

Some other words you'll find it hard to do without are '<u>this</u>' and '<u>these</u>'.
They're called <u>demonstrative adjectives</u>, if you're interested in the technical terms.

The French word for 'these' is '**ces**'

The word for 'this' changes to match the thing you're talking about — depending on whether
it's <u>masculine</u> or <u>feminine</u>. Learn this table:

masculine singular	masculine singular before vowel or silent 'h'	feminine singular	plural
ce	*cet*	*cette*	*ces*

Examples

ce stylo = this pen

cet élève = this pupil

cette maison = this house

ces pommes = these apples

Watch out for **masculine** words that start with a **vowel**

If a <u>masculine</u> word starts with a <u>vowel</u> (<u>a</u>, <u>e</u>, <u>i</u>, <u>o</u> or <u>u</u>) or a silent '<u>h</u>', then you use '<u>cet</u>'.

Cet élève est sympa. = This pupil is nice.

This doesn't apply to feminine words, even if they start with a vowel.

Cette écharpe est chère. = This scarf is expensive.

Don't ignore these just because they're little words
Sometimes it's handy that words are masculine or feminine in French. You can't tell if 'this
pupil' is a boy or a girl, but 'cet élève' is a boy, and 'cette élève' is a girl. Useful sometimes.

'Tu'

In French, there are two ways of saying you — 'tu' and 'vous'.
It sounds tricky, but if you follow these simple rules, you'll get it right.

Use '**tu**' for a friend or close relative

This is how you'd ask your friend or a
relative like your dad to the cinema:

> *Est-ce que tu veux aller au cinéma?* = Do you want to go to the cinema?

Use '**tu**' for someone your age or younger

This is how you'd ask the name of a French
person who's your age or younger:

> *Comment tu t'appelles?* = What are you called?

Use '**tu**' for talking to an animal or pet

This is how you'd ask your dog if he's hungry:

> *Est-ce que tu as faim?* = Are you hungry?

Say '**please**' to someone you call 'tu' — '**S'il te plaît**'

If you call someone 'tu', then you need to say
's'il te plaît' for 'please'.

> *Tu peux fermer la porte, s'il te plaît?* = Can you shut the door, please?

At last, some pretty simple stuff
You probably already knew about saying 'tu' to your mates and 'vous' to the teacher. But make
sure you get it right when you're doing role plays and things. It's easy to make a mistake.

'Vous'

'Vous' is a bit of a tricky one, because it can be used for <u>one person</u>, or for <u>lots</u> of people. It's also easy to get <u>confused</u> and use '<u>tu</u>' to the teacher in an oral exam, so watch out.

Use '**vous**' for **two or more** people

This is how your <u>teacher</u> will speak to the class, using '<u>vous</u>':

Qu'est-ce que vous avez fait le week-end?

= What did you do at the weekend?

Use '**vous**' for an older person you **don't know well**

You should use '<u>vous</u>' for talking to an <u>older person</u> who's not a friend or close relative, or to someone you <u>don't know</u> very well.

Où habitez-vous?   = Where do you live?

Use '**vous**' to be **polite**

If you follow the rule above about <u>older people</u> and <u>strangers</u>, you'll be <u>polite</u>. But sometimes it's a bit hard to know which to use. If you're talking to someone like your penfriend's dad, then you should definitely use 'vous' when you talk to them, although your penfriend probably won't. If he <u>asks</u> you to use '<u>tu</u>' instead, then that's fine.

> Don't forget — your teacher will use '<u>vous</u>' when they're talking to the class, and '<u>tu</u>' when they're just talking to you.
>
> You should use '<u>vous</u>' for talking to your teacher, because they're (a lot) older than you, and because it's <u>polite</u>.

Vous and tu is simple once you know it
Ages ago people used 'vous' for anyone they didn't know. Nowadays that's changed, and you can get away with 'tu' for anyone who's fairly young. If you're not sure, just use 'vous'.

Practice Questions

1   Copy out these sentences and fill in the gaps with the correct form of the adjective in brackets. The first one has been done for you. (NB It might not always need changing.)

a)   J'ai une ....*grande*............ (grand) maison.

b)   Il a des yeux .... (vert).

c)   Elles sont .... (petit).

d)   Ton père est .... (gentil).

e)   Dans mon collège il y a beaucoup de .... (beau) filles.

f)   Ma grand-mère est une .... (vieux) femme.

2   Copy out these sentences and fill in the gaps. The bits in brackets tell you what to write. The first one has been done for you.

a)   Tom est grand, mais Mark est .....*plus grand*..... (taller).

b)   Sophie est belle, mais Marie est .... (prettier).

c)   Suresh est mince, mais Frank est .... (thinner).

d)   Ton père est gentil, mais mon père est .... (kinder).

3   Use the phrases in the box to write out the following sentences in French. (Hint: use 'mieux que' with verbs, and use 'meilleur que' with nouns.)

| mieux que   meilleur que   pire que |

a)   The book is better than the film. ....

b)   French is worse than German. ....

c)   I dance better than you. ....

d)   My dad is better than your dad. ....

Practice Questions

4 Copy out these sentences and fill in the gaps with the correct possessive adjective. The letter in brackets shows if the word is masculine or feminine. Use the table on page 129 to help you.

a) My brother is 15. .... frère (m) a 15 ans.

b) Her car is red. .... voiture (f) est rouge.

c) Your dog is nasty. .... chien (m) est méchant.

d) I ate his sandwich. J'ai mangé .... sandwich (m).

e) There are 200 pupils at my school. Il y a 200 élèves dans .... collège (m).

f) His sister hates your brother. .... soeur (f) déteste .... frère (m).

g) Where are your socks? Où sont .... chaussettes (f, pl)?

5 Copy out these sentences and change 'un', 'une' or 'des' to the correct French word for 'this' or 'these' — **ce**, **cet**, **cette** or **ces**.

a) une souris

b) des chaussures

c) un stylo

d) un enfant

e) une glace

f) un fromage

g) une orange

h) des chiens

i) un hôpital

6 Write down how you would do the following in French, remembering to use the correct word for 'you' — either '**tu**' or '**vous**'. You might need the right word for 'your' as well — look at pages 129, 131 and 132 if you get stuck.

a) Ask your dog if he's hungry.

b) Ask someone on the street if they speak English.

c) Ask a new classmate what their name is.

d) Tell your teacher that you hate her lessons.

e) Tell your friend that you like her shoes.

Verbs in the Present Tense

You need to know a few <u>grammatical terms</u> here — you just can't get away from them.

The <u>verbs</u> you've come across, like 'manger', 'jouer', 'faire', are all in the <u>infinitive</u> — that's the form of the verb that you find in the <u>dictionary</u>.

The infinitive is made of a '<u>stem</u>' and the '<u>ending</u>'.

The **present** tense is what's **happening now**

The <u>rule</u> to form the <u>present tense</u> is to add the <u>endings</u> below (and on the next page) onto the <u>stem</u>.

There are <u>3</u> types of regular verbs: verbs ending in -<u>er</u>, -<u>ir</u>, -<u>re</u>.

Here are some examples of present tense stems for verbs ending in -<u>er</u>, -<u>ir</u> and -<u>re</u>.

infinitive	regarder	finir	vendre
stem	regard-	fin-	vend-

Endings for **-er** verbs

To form the present tense of <u>regular</u> '-er' verbs, add the following endings to the verb's stem:

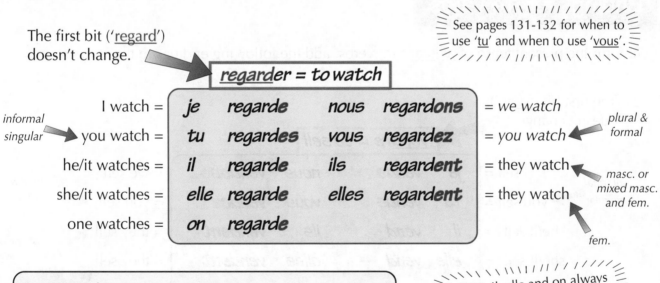

The first bit ('<u>regard</u>') doesn't change.

See pages 131-132 for when to use '<u>tu</u>' and when to use '<u>vous</u>'.

<u>regarder</u> = to watch

				= we watch
I watch =	je	regarde	nous regardons	= we watch
you watch =	tu	regardes	vous regardez	= you watch
he/it watches =	il	regarde	ils regardent	= they watch
she/it watches =	elle	regarde	elles regardent	= they watch
one watches =	on	regarde		

informal singular

plural & formal

masc. or mixed masc. and fem.

fem.

For example:
To say something like 'He <u>watches</u> TV' is dead easy:

1) Start by <u>knocking off</u> the '<u>er</u>': regarder
2) Then <u>add on</u> the <u>new ending</u>: regard e
3) And — <u>ta da</u>... Il <u>regarde</u> la télévision.

NOTE: <u>il</u>, <u>elle</u> and <u>on</u> always have the <u>same</u> ending.

NOTE: if '<u>they</u>' refers to a mixed group of males <u>and</u> females, you use '<u>ils</u>'.

This is important stuff

If you want to take French for GCSE later on, it's vitally important that you learn this stuff. Getting your verbs right is one of the things you'll get the most marks for. So learn this well.

Verbs in the Present Tense

Here's how to form the present tense of -ir and -re verbs.

Endings for -ir verbs

To form the present tense of <u>regular</u> '-ir' verbs, add the following endings to the verb's stem:

The first bit ('<u>fin</u>') doesn't change.

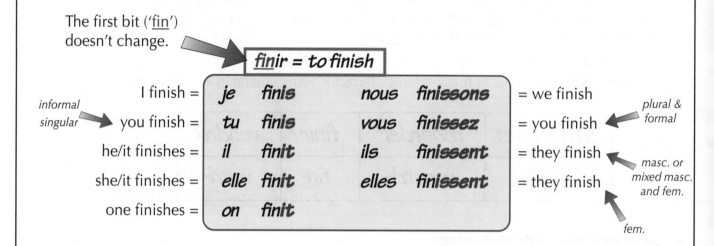

finir = to finish

I finish =	*je*	*finis*	*nous*	*finissons*	= we finish
you finish =	*tu*	*finis*	*vous*	*finissez*	= you finish
he/it finishes =	*il*	*finit*	*ils*	*finissent*	= they finish
she/it finishes =	*elle*	*finit*	*elles*	*finissent*	= they finish
one finishes =	*on*	*finit*			

informal singular

plural & formal

masc. or mixed masc. and fem.

fem.

Endings for -re verbs

To form the present tense of <u>regular</u> '-re' verbs, add the following endings to the verb's stem:

The first bit ('<u>vend</u>') doesn't change.

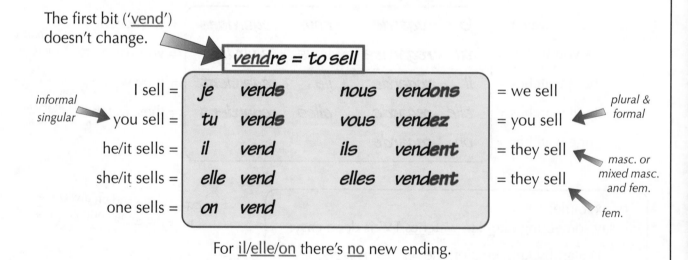

vendre = to sell

I sell =	*je*	*vends*	*nous*	*vendons*	= we sell
you sell =	*tu*	*vends*	*vous*	*vendez*	= you sell
he/it sells =	*il*	*vend*	*ils*	*vendent*	= they sell
she/it sells =	*elle*	*vend*	*elles*	*vendent*	= they sell
one sells =	*on*	*vend*			

informal singular

plural & formal

masc. or mixed masc. and fem.

fem.

For <u>il</u>/<u>elle</u>/<u>on</u> there's <u>no</u> new ending.

See p.137 for the <u>irregular</u> verbs.

Think this is confusing? Wait for the irregular verbs

The only way of learning this stuff is just practising it over and over again, and testing yourself until you know it. And once you do know it, you'll be the envy of all your friends, just wait.

Verbs in the Present Tense

Hmmm — <u>irregular verbs</u>. Not the best way to start the day...

Learn these three **irregular verbs**

An '<u>irregular verb</u>' is a verb that <u>doesn't follow</u> the normal pattern of regular verbs.
Unfortunately, some of the <u>most useful</u> verbs are irregular... (typical).
Here are the <u>three</u> that you can't do without.

① '<u>Être</u>' means '<u>to be</u>' — it's probably the <u>most important</u> verb in the world... ever. So learn it.

être = to be

I am =	**je**	**suis**	**nous**	**sommes**	= we are
you (inf. sing.) are =	**tu**	**es**	**vous**	**êtes**	= you (pl. & f.) are
he/she/one/it is =	**il/elle/on**	**est**	**ils/elles**	**sont**	= they are

② You'll need this verb loads — '<u>avoir</u>' ('<u>to have</u>').
It's <u>easy</u> to learn, so there's no excuse.

avoir = to have

I have =	**j'**	**ai**	**nous**	**avons**	= we have
you (inf. sing.) have =	**tu**	**as**	**vous**	**avez**	= you (pl. & f.) have
he/she/one/it has =	**il/elle/on**	**a**	**ils/elles**	**ont**	= they have

③ '<u>Aller</u>' ('<u>to go</u>'). Useful to say where you're going, and what you're going to do (see pages 145-146).

aller = to go

I go =	**je**	**vais**	**nous**	**allons**	= we go
you (inf. sing.) go =	**tu**	**vas**	**vous**	**allez**	= you (pl. & f.) go
he/she/one/it goes =	**il/elle/on**	**va**	**ils/elles**	**vont**	= they go

Just learn them, they're not that bad

Why did whoever invented French choose to invent irregular verbs? I don't get it. Why didn't he or she just make all verbs end the same way and be easy to learn? What a load of hassle.

'There is' and 'It is'

You're not going to get very far at describing things if you can't say 'there is' and 'it is'.

There is = 'il y a'

'Il y a' is how you say 'there is' or 'there are' in French. You might have noticed that it takes a form of the irregular verb 'avoir', which you met on the last page. But then again, you might not have noticed and it doesn't matter really.

Here are some examples of 'il y a' in action:

Dans ma ville il y a un parc.   = In my town there is a park.

Il y a trois chats dans le jardin.   = There are three cats in the garden.

Chez moi il y a cinq salles.   = In my house there are five rooms.

It is = 'c'est'

'C'est' is how you say 'it is' in French. This phrase takes a form of the irregular verb 'être', which you also met on the last page. 'C'est' is really important — you'll find that you can't get very far in the world of French without using this little beauty.

Here are some examples of sentences which use 'c'est':

C'est très intéressant!   = It's very interesting!

C'est bon, mais le français est meilleur.   = It's good, but French is better.

C'est sur la table.   = It's on the table.

Il y a un livre CGP pour français KS3 — c'est magnifique
This page isn't as tricky as the last few — a bit of welcome light-relief for you. However, it should show you how often the verbs 'être' and 'avoir' crop up. They're all over the place.

Verbs with 'se' in Front

As if the irregular verbs weren't bad enough, now you have to learn about verbs with 'se' in front. Poor you, you have my utmost sympathy.

Verbs with 'se' — **se lever**, **se laver**, **s'habiller**...

1) Some verbs in French have '<u>se</u>' in front. The '<u>se</u>' bit means '<u>self</u>'.
Seems a bit odd saying things like '<u>I get myself up</u>' and
'<u>I wake myself up</u>', but that's the way it works in French.

2) Learn this list of the <u>most useful</u> 'se' verbs.
You mainly use them to talk about your <u>daily routine</u>.

For all you grammar fans, these are called '<u>reflexive verbs</u>'.

se réveiller = to wake up

se lever = to get up

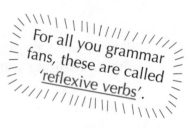

WATCH OUT: se l<u>e</u>ver and se l<u>a</u>ver look similar, but they mean <u>totally different</u> things.

se laver = to have a wash

se doucher = to have a shower

s'habiller = to get dressed

se coucher = to go to bed

Have a look at the next page for how to put reflexive verbs into action.

To go to bed... if only

No skulking off to bed just yet. You haven't quite learned enough about reflexive verbs yet.
Turn the page to find out how to say 'I go to bed', 'you wake up', 'we get dressed' etc.

Verbs with 'se' in Front

These 'se' (reflexive) verbs are a bit special and just slightly tricky.
Trouble is, you use them a lot — head down, get 'em learned, get 'em right.

People doing stuff — **Je me lève**, je me lave...

1) If you've read the last page, then so far, so good. But that 'se' bit is for the
infinitive (see p. 135). You need different words instead of 'se' when you use
these verbs with 'je', 'tu', 'elle', etc...

2) I'll bet you've already come across this, maybe
without realising you were using a reflexive verb:

je m'appelle   comes from →   **s'appeler**

= I am called   = to be called / named

3) Look at the box below. You can see all the little words to use instead of 'se'.
I've used 'se lever' as an example, but these words work for any 'se' verb.
Learn them off by heart.

se lever = to get up

I get up =   **je me lève**   **nous nous levons**   = we get up

you (inf. sing.) get up =   **tu te lèves**   **vous vous levez**   = you (pl. & f.) get up

he/she/one/ it gets up =   **il/elle/on se lève**   **ils/elles se lèvent**   = they get up

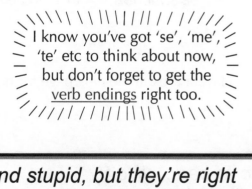

I know you've got 'se', 'me',
'te' etc to think about now,
but don't forget to get the
verb endings right too.

'Nous nous' and 'vous vous' may sound stupid, but they're right
So don't go saying 'nous levons' instead of 'nous nous levons', because you'd be wrong.
Actually, come to think of it, 'nous nous' reminds me of that teletubby hoover thing. Hmmm.

Practice Questions

1   Write these sentences out in French. The French verbs to use are in the brackets. The verbs follow the same pattern as 'vendre' — it's written out below to remind you.

a)   I understand. *[comprendre]*

b)   You (sing. informal) lose. *[perdre]*

c)   He takes. *[prendre]*

d)   We go down. *[descendre]*

e)   You (formal) wait. *[attendre]*

f)   They bite. *[mordre]*

Vendre	
Je	vends
Tu	vends
Il/elle	vend
Nous	vendons
Vous	vendez
Ils/elles	vendent

2   Copy and complete these sentences by filling in the right form of the verb in the brackets. I've done the first one for you.

a)   Je suis. Nous ..*sommes*. *[être]*

b)   Je vais. Nous .... *[aller]*

c)   Il a. Ils .... *[avoir]*

d)   Tu es. Vous .... *[être]*

e)   J'ai. Nous .... *[avoir]*

f)   Tu vas. Vous .... *[aller]*

g)   Elle est. Elles .... *[être]*

h)   Tu as. Vous .... *[avoir]*

Track 18   Listening Question

3   Your new French penfriend, Claude, tells you some information about his family. Listen to what he says and then answer the questions below.

a)   How old is Claude?

b)   What is his brother called?

c)   How old is his brother?

d)   What is his sister called?

e)   What relation to him is Marie?

f)   What type of animal is their pet?

4   Now write these out in French:

a)   I'm English.

b)   I'm 13 years old.

c)   I have a dog.

d)   Claude has a sister.

Practice Questions

5 Copy these sentences, choosing either **_il y a_** or **_c'est_**, whichever is correct.

  a) J'aime le football, **il y a / c'est** intéressant.

  b) J'habite à Paris, **il y a / c'est** beaucoup de cinémas.

  c) **Il y a / C'est** un chat dans le jardin.

  d) Je déteste faire les courses, **il y a / c'est** très ennuyeux.

6 Using the pictures, write (in French) what Bobo does at different times of the day. I've done the first one for you.

  a)  *07:00*

  Bobo se réveille.

  b) *07:30*

  c) *07:35*

  d) *07:45*

  e) *19:45*

7 Copy and complete these sentences using the reflexive pronouns from the box. (One of them is used twice.)

  a) Elle .... lève.

  b) Nous .... couchons.

  c) Je .... réveille.

  d) Vous .... appelez.

te	vous	se
m'	nous	me

  e) Ils .... lavent.

  f) Tu .... douches.

  g) Je .... appelle.

How to Make Sentences Negative

'Can't get you out of my head', 'I can't live, if living is without you' — pop would be nothing without negatives. And, er... they come up in loads of phrases in French too, surprise surprise.

Use 'ne ... pas' to say 'not'

1)   In English you change a sentence to mean the opposite by adding 'not'.

    EXAMPLE: *I am English.*   ➡   *I am not English.*

2)   In French, you have to add two little words, 'ne' and 'pas'.
    They go on either side of the action word (the verb).

    EXAMPLE: *Je suis anglais.*   ➡   *Je ne suis pas anglais.*

        = I am English.

        'Suis' is the verb. The 'ne' goes
        in front, and the 'pas' goes after.

        = I am not English.

3)   In front of a word that starts with a vowel, the ne changes to n'.

    EXAMPLE: *Je n'aime pas les chiens.*

                = I don't like dogs.

Just add 'ne' and 'pas' — easy
So — as a quick recap... Take a simple French sentence (e.g. Je mange les bananes). To make it negative, just add a 'ne' and a 'pas' around the verb (e.g. Je ne mange pas les bananes).

How to make Sentences Negative

It's all very well to make sentences negative by adding a 'ne' and a 'pas', but there are other more complex things you can do... As well as 'not', you can say 'never' and 'nothing'. Wow.

never = 'ne ... jamais'

To start with, here's '<u>never</u>':

ne ... jamais = never

As with 'ne... pas', the two words go on <u>either side</u> of the <u>verb</u>.

FOR EXAMPLE: *Je ne vais jamais en vacances.*   = I <u>never</u> go on holiday.

Je n'écoute jamais la radio.   = I <u>never</u> listen to the radio.

Je ne mange jamais de jambon.   = I <u>never</u> eat ham.

nothing = 'ne ... rien'

ne ... rien = nothing

FOR EXAMPLE: *Je ne mange rien le matin.*   = I don't eat anything in the morning.

(Literally: I eat <u>nothing</u> in the morning.)

Je n' ai rien vu.   = I saw <u>nothing</u>.

(See pages 149-150 for more verbs in the past tense.)

Just remember to put the 'ne...jamais' or 'ne...rien' around the verb
It's easy to make a mistake with this stuff and put the 'ne...jamais' or 'ne...rien' around the wrong bit. Don't go writing 'je n'ai vu rien', for example, because that's just not right.

Talking about the Future

Making arrangements, talking about holiday plans...
It's all stuff you're <u>going to</u> do, for which (you've guessed it) you need this page. Read on.

What is the **future tense**?

1) You use the <u>future tense</u> to talk about events that are <u>going to happen</u>... in the <u>future</u>.

2) There are <u>two ways</u> to form the future tense.
The good news is that you <u>only</u> have to learn the <u>easy one</u> now.

(The hard way can wait till GCSE.)

You can use '**I'm going to**' to talk about the future

1) This is the <u>easiest way</u> to talk about the future.

2) All you need is the <u>infinitive</u> of the verb you want,
and the <u>present tense</u> of the verb '<u>aller</u>' (to go).

3) You should already know the 'aller' bits. Sorted. If not, see p.137.

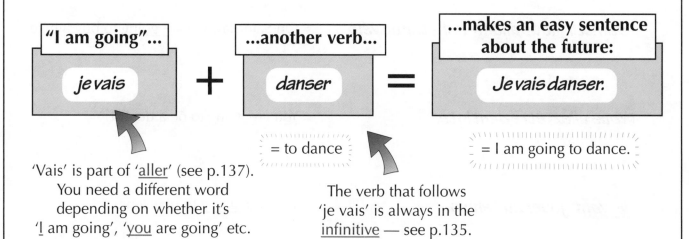

"I am going"... + ...another verb... = **...makes an easy sentence about the future:**

je vais + *danser* = *Je vais danser.*

= to dance

= I am going to dance.

'Vais' is part of '<u>aller</u>' (see p.137).
You need a different word
depending on whether it's
'<u>I</u> am going', '<u>you</u> are going' etc.

The verb that follows
'je vais' is always in the
<u>infinitive</u> — see p.135.

Use the future tense to talk about your plans

What could be easier? I'm going to blah. You're going to blah. <u>Make sure</u> you've got it <u>sorted</u>:
Put this into French: *a) On Saturday, I'm going to play football. b) He's going to go to France.**

*a) Samedi, je vais jouer au football. b) Il va aller en France.

Talking about the Future

Now it's time for a shed-load of examples, just so you get the idea about the future tense.

Here are your **future tense examples**

Lucky for you, these examples all start in different ways. So now you can say '<u>I'm</u> going to', '<u>you're</u> going to', '<u>they're</u> going to' etc. You've <u>no excuse</u> now not to talk about the future.

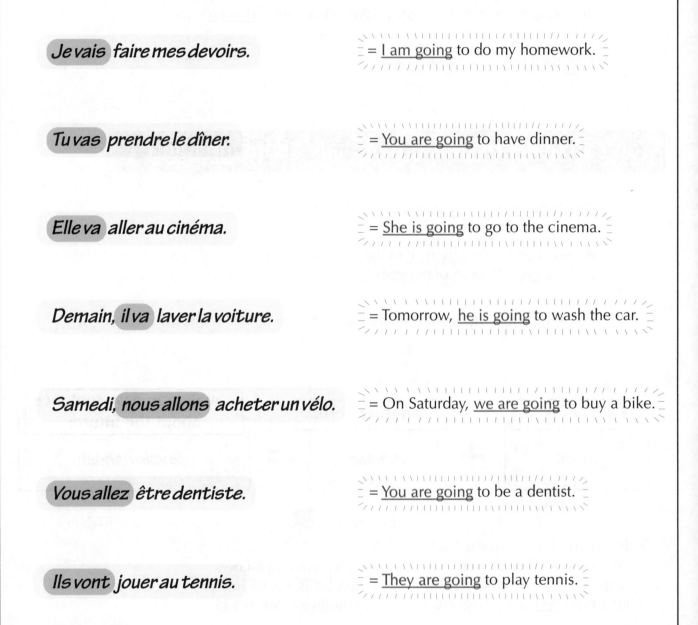

Je vais faire mes devoirs.　　　= <u>I am going</u> to do my homework.

Tu vas prendre le dîner.　　　= <u>You are going</u> to have dinner.

Elle va aller au cinéma.　　　= <u>She is going</u> to go to the cinema.

Demain, **il va** laver la voiture.　　　= Tomorrow, <u>he is going</u> to wash the car.

Samedi, **nous allons** acheter un vélo.　　　= On Saturday, <u>we are going</u> to buy a bike.

Vous allez être dentiste.　　　= <u>You are going</u> to be a dentist.

Ils vont jouer au tennis.　　　= <u>They are going</u> to play tennis.

Phew! What a lot of examples

So, what you've got to do is take 'I'm going' or 'you're going' or whatever you want to say, and just add an infinitive on the end. Hey presto — an instant future tense sentence.

Giving People Orders

Here's how to <u>boss people about</u> — excellent. Although it has to be said that, most of the time, you need these to <u>understand</u> when <u>other people</u> are telling <u>you</u> what to do. Unfair, eh?

How to **boss people about**

1) It's dead easy to give people orders in French. All you need is <u>the present tense</u> (see pages 135-137), but you <u>remove</u> the 'tu' or 'vous' bits.

   For example, instead of saying 'vous écoutez'
   (you listen), you say 'écoutez!' (listen!).

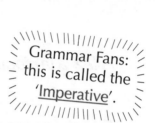
Grammar Fans: this is called the 'Imperative'.

2) The only thing you need to remember is whether you should be using the ending for '<u>tu</u>' <u>or</u> '<u>vous</u>'. Check pages 131-132 if you can't quite remember the rule.

   FOR EXAMPLE:

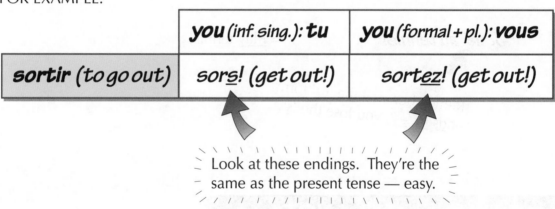

	you *(inf. sing.)*: **tu**	**you** *(formal + pl.)*: **vous**
sortir *(to go out)*	*sor<u>s</u>! (get out!)*	*sort<u>ez</u>! (get out!)*

   Look at these endings. They're the same as the present tense — easy.

3) There is an odd-one-out... (typical). If the '<u>tu</u>' form <u>ends in</u> '<u>es</u>', you lose the '<u>s</u>'.

   FOR EXAMPLE: *Mange tes légumes!*   = Eat your vegetables!

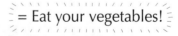

   The 'tu' form of manger is actually '<u>manges</u>', so we knock off the '<u>s</u>'.

Learn this! Learn the rest! Learn it all! Then clean your room!
This is simple — just lose the 'tu' and 'vous' bits. And remember that spelling rule for the 's'.
Of course, if you're speaking the orders, you can relax, because you can't hear the 's' anyway.

Giving People Orders

Here's a bit more on giving people orders. In particular, you'll learn how to tell people <u>not</u> to do things, which is always useful. Don't do that, don't worry, don't pick your nose etc.

Here are some **examples** of **orders**

Firstly, here are some examples of orders using the '<u>vous</u>' form:

Allez à la piscine! = <u>Go</u> to the swimming pool!

Regardez la télévision! = <u>Watch</u> the television!

Now, here are some examples of orders using the '<u>tu</u>' form:

Finis tes devoirs! = <u>Finish</u> your homework!

Joue au tennis! = <u>Play</u> tennis!

Remember — if the '<u>tu</u>' form <u>ends in</u> '<u>es</u>', you lose the '<u>s</u>'.

How to tell people what **NOT** to do

To tell people <u>not</u> to do something, you need to use the words '<u>ne</u>' and '<u>pas</u>' (see pages 143-144). Put '<u>ne</u>' at the <u>front</u>, and '<u>pas</u>' at the <u>end</u>.

FOR EXAMPLE:

Ne sors pas!

Ne jouez pas au football!

= <u>Don't</u> go out!

= <u>Don't</u> play football!

Orders are pretty easy to learn
Luckily, this isn't too hard to learn. You can only ever boss people around in the 'tu' or 'vous' forms, so there are only two different possible endings to learn. I'm sure you can handle that.

Talking about the Past

You use the <u>past tense</u> to talk about things that have <u>already happened</u>... *in the past*. You only have to learn the past tense of <u>regular</u> verbs (verbs that always follow the same pattern).

The **past tense** is for talking about the **past**...

Here's how you make the past tense.
There are <u>two</u> important bits.

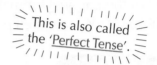
This is also called the '<u>Perfect Tense</u>'.

J'ai **joué** *au tennis.* = I played tennis.

1) You always need a bit to mean '<u>I have</u>'. In <u>English</u>, you don't always need the 'have' bit, like in 'last week, I played tennis'. BUT in <u>French</u> you <u>must</u> use the 'have' bit.

2) This bit means '<u>played</u>'. It's a <u>special version</u> of 'jouer' (to play). In English, most of these words end in '-ed'.

From the example above, you can see that there are <u>two parts</u> to the perfect tense — the '<u>avoir</u>' part and the <u>special past tense words</u> (see the next page).

Past tense **part 1 — avoir** (to have)

For the '<u>have</u>' bit of past tense phrases, you use the <u>present tense</u> of '<u>avoir</u>' (see p.137).

| EXAMPLES: |

<u>*Tu as*</u> *mangé une banane.* = <u>You have</u> eaten a banana.

<u>*Nous avons*</u> *mangé une banane.* = <u>We have</u> eaten a banana.

You use the past tense loads when you speak — it's really important
I bet you've never really thought about the past tense before, have you? You talk about the past in English all the time, but you never realised that adding 'ed' to words made them past tense.

Talking about the Past

In English, we just tend to add an 'ed' on to words to put them into the past tense.
However, in French, there are <u>three</u> different ways to put words into the past tense.

Past tense **part 2 — special past tense words**

Learn the <u>patterns</u> for making the special past tense words like '<u>joué</u>' (played).
These words are called <u>past participles</u>, by the way.

-er verbs

FORMULA: **Remove '<u>-er</u>', then add '<u>é</u>'**

EXAMPLES:

jou<u>er</u> → *jou<u>é</u>*
to play   played

parl<u>er</u> → *parl<u>é</u>*
to talk   talked

-ir verbs

FORMULA: **Remove '<u>-r</u>'**

EXAMPLES:

fini<u>r</u> → *fini*
to finish   finished

choisi<u>r</u> → *choisi*
to choose   chosen

-re verbs

FORMULA: **Remove '<u>-re</u>', then add '<u>u</u>'**

EXAMPLES:

vend<u>re</u> → *vend<u>u</u>*
to sell   sold

attend<u>re</u> → *attend<u>u</u>*
to wait   waited

Remember the 'avoir' though

It's all very well remembering how to put each type of verb into the past tense, but don't forget
to put the 'avoir' part in there too. So it's NOT 'je fini', but it IS 'j'<u>ai</u> fini'. Don't forget.

Practice Questions

Track 19   Listening Question

1   Listen to the description of Jean-Pierre, and then tick the
     boxes to show whether the statements are true or false.

		TRUE	FALSE
a)	Jean-Pierre isn't from Paris.	☐	☐
b)	He is 17 years old.	☐	☐
c)	He likes music.	☐	☐
d)	He has a cat and a dog.	☐	☐
e)	He likes bananas.	☐	☐
f)	He has a brother.	☐	☐

2   I've written out these positive sentences — you have to write
     out the negative sentences. I've done the first one for you.

   a) I get up at 6 o'clock. = Je me lève à six heures.
       I do **not** get up at 6 o'clock.   *= Je ne me lève pas à six heures.*

   b) I am French = Je suis français.
       I'm **not** French.

   c) You eat at midday. = Tu manges à midi.
       You eat **nothing** at midday.

   d) We talk in class. = Nous parlons en classe.
       We **never** talk in class.

3   Copy and complete these French sentences. The bits in brackets tell you what to say.

   a) *[We are going]* jouer au tennis.

   b) *[He is going]* préparer le dîner.

   c) *[They are going]* aller au cinéma.

   d) *[I am going]* acheter une glace.

   e) *[You are going]* te coucher.

Practice Questions

4 Write down what these signs mean in English.

a)

b)

c)

d)

e)

f)

5 Copy and complete these French sentences. You're talking to friends, so use the "tu" version of the command. We've put the infinitives in brackets to help you.

a) Walk more quickly! = ... plus vite! [marcher]

b) Eat your dinner! = ... ton dîner! [manger]

c) Play quietly! = ... doucement! [jouer]

d) Don't fall! = Ne .... pas! [tomber]

6 Rewrite this story in the past tense. The words you'll need to change are underlined. To give you a hand, we've listed the infinitives of the verbs at the end.

> À neuf heures je <u>téléphone</u> à mon ami Henri, et nous <u>décidons</u> d'aller au centre-ville. Je <u>marche</u> au centre à pied, mais mon ami <u>choisit</u> l'autobus. Nous <u>regardons</u> les boutiques et nous <u>achetons</u> un CD et des glaces. Après, nous <u>jouons</u> au tennis de table.

téléphoner   décider   marcher   choisir   regarder   acheter   jouer

7 Imagine this was your timetable for yesterday, and write sentences to say what you did at each time. The first one has been done for you.

a) 8.00   manger une banane   *J'ai mangé une banane.*

b) 9.00   commencer les cours

c) 10.45 parler avec mes amis

d) 12.30 déjeuner

e) 3.30   jouer au tennis

I Want, I Can

Vouloir and pouvoir have two things in common. They're usually followed by another verb, and they're a bit weird.

Pouvoir — to be able to / can

Learn how to use this verb properly, because it comes up all the time.

I can =	*je peux*
you (inf. singular) can =	*tu peux*
he/she/it/one can =	*il/elle/on peut*
we can =	*nous pouvons*
you (formal/plural) can =	*vous pouvez*
they can =	*ils/elles peuvent*

Tu peux sortir ce soir? = Can you go out tonight?

Elles peuvent rester demain. = They can stay tomorrow.

Vouloir — to want

This is another really handy verb that follows the same pattern as 'pouvoir':

I want =	*je veux*
you (inf. singular) want =	*tu veux*
he / she / it / one wants =	*il/elle/on veut*
we want =	*nous voulons*
you (formal / plural) want =	*vous voulez*
they want =	*ils/elles veulent*

Vouloir and pouvoir are usually followed by an infinitive (see p.135). All the underlined words are infinitives.

Je veux aller au cinéma. = I want to go to the cinema.

Nous voulons partir. = We want to leave.

*You might not **want** to, but you **can** learn this if you try...*
Look at 'pouvoir'. Read through all the bits. Cover it up and write it out from memory. Check you got it right, and keep going till you do. Then do the same for 'vouloir' — it's the only way.

I Must, I Like

Once you've got the hang of <u>vouloir</u> and <u>pouvoir</u>, try learning <u>devoir</u>.
It follows the same <u>pattern</u>, and it's also pretty useful.

Devoir — to have to / must

'<u>Devoir</u>' is usually followed by an <u>infinitive</u> (see p. 135), just like 'vouloir' and 'pouvoir'.

I must =	*je dois*
you (inf. singular) must =	*tu dois*
he/she/it/one must =	*il/elle/on doit*
we must =	*nous devons*
you (formal/plural) must =	*vous devez*
they must =	*ils/elles doivent*

On doit <u>arriver</u> tôt.   = We (one) must arrive early.

Vous devez <u>avoir</u> faim!   = You must be hungry!

Aimer — to like / love

<u>Aimer</u> is another very useful verb that's followed by the infinitive.
This is a '<u>regular</u>' verb — see pages 135-136.

I like / love =	*j'aime*
you (inf. singular) like / love =	*tu aimes*
he/she/it/one likes / loves =	*il/elle/on aime*
we like / love =	*nous aimons*
you (formal/plural) like / love =	*vous aimez*
they like / love =	*ils/elles aiment*

J'aime <u>jouer</u> au football.   = I like playing football.

Tu aimes <u>sortir</u>?   = Do you like going out?

Je dois faire mes révisions

Learning to put infinitives after verbs is a really important step in learning French. Once you can do that, you can make extremely complex sentences and properly impress French people.

Useful Small Words

There are <u>three</u> useful small words on this page, and they crop up pretty much <u>everywhere</u>.

Use 'à' to say 'to' or 'at'

'<u>à</u>' is a really useful word. Use it to say that you're going <u>to</u> a place.

Je vais à la piscine. = I'm going <u>to</u> the swimming pool.

Elle va au cinéma. = She's going <u>to</u> the cinema.

Ils vont aux États-Unis. = They're going <u>to</u> the USA.

> *Don't forget, 'à' changes to 'au' for masculine words, and 'aux' for plurals.*

'de' means 'of' or 'from'

1) Where you use '<u>of</u>' in English, you usually use '<u>de</u>' in French. You use it for quantities.

Une bouteille de lait. = A bottle <u>of</u> milk.

Un paquet de biscuits. = A packet <u>of</u> biscuits.

2) To say '<u>from</u>', you use 'de' as well. You need this to say where you come from, for example.

Je viens de Paris. = I come <u>from</u> Paris.

> *Remember, 'de' is also used to say 'some'.*

'pour' means 'for'

'<u>Pour</u>' is a really handy little word for '<u>for</u>'.

Elle a une robe pour moi. = She has a dress <u>for</u> me.

Le train pour Avignon. = The train <u>for</u> Avignon.

They're small but perfectly formed

Or at least they will be perfectly formed once you've learnt how to use them. They're not particularly complicated, but you need to be careful to use 'à', 'au' or 'aux' correctly.

Useful Small Words

There are a lot of little words that you need for saying where things are in relation to each other.

Learn these words for **where** things are

Use these words for talking about where things are in your house or bedroom,
or for giving directions.

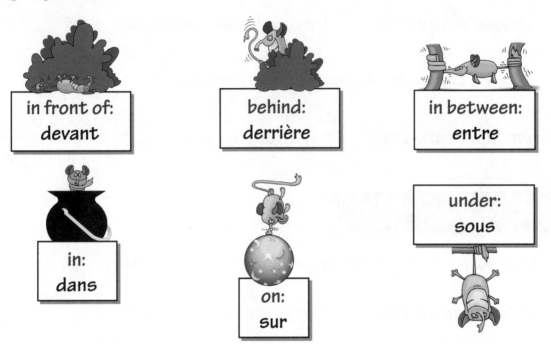

in front of:	behind:	in between:
devant	**derrière**	**entre**

in:	on:	under:
dans	**sur**	**sous**

Mon ordinateur est sur *la table.*   = My computer is on the table.

Le cinéma est entre *la poste et l'hôtel.*   = The cinema is between the post office and the hotel.

Some of these words **change**

Some of these words for saying where things are change, depending on whether the word after them is masculine, feminine or plural (see page 121).

en face de: opposite
à côté de: next to

Le café est en face du *cinéma.*

= The café is opposite the cinema.

My brain is somewhere between the cinema and the chip shop
Directions are something that French teachers just love to talk about. The way they go on about it, you'd think that everyone in France was permanently lost. Have they never heard of maps?

Small Linking Words

Learn these linking words — they're really useful for linking phrases together and building longer sentences. The technical term for these joining words is <u>conjunctions</u>.

And — et

Pour le petit-déjeuner, je mange du pain.

AND

Pour le petit-déjeuner, je mange des céréales.

= I eat bread for breakfast.

= I eat cereal for breakfast.

Pour le petit-déjeuner, je mange du pain ET des céréales.

= I eat bread AND cereal for breakfast.

Or — ou

Elle mange un sandwich à midi.

OR

Elle mange de la pizza à midi.

= She eats a sandwich at lunchtime.

= She eats some pizza at lunchtime.

Elle mange un sandwich OU de la pizza à midi.

= She eats a sandwich or some pizza at lunchtime.

Linking words help you sound a lot better at French

If you use these linking words, you'll be talking in joined-up sentences, which sounds a lot more realistic than saying things like 'My brother is 15. He likes football. He likes girls.'

Small Linking Words

And... slightly more complex than 'and' and 'or'... are 'but' and 'because'. Hooray.

But — **mais**

J'aime jouer au football.   BUT   **Je n'aime pas jouer au rugby.**

= I like playing football.   = I don't like playing rugby.

J'aime jouer au football MAIS je n'aime pas jouer au rugby.

= I like playing football but I don't like playing rugby.

Because — **parce que**

J'aime le français parce que **c'est intéressant.**

= I like French because it's interesting.

Je déteste le shopping parce que **c'est ennuyeux.**

= I hate shopping because it's boring.

Nous aimons le shopping parce que c'est amusant.

So now you can say 'Yeah, but, no, but' in French... How useful
Just try going a whole day without saying 'and', 'or', 'but' or 'because'. You'd be pretty limited in what you could actually say. And you'd sound stupid, so nobody would talk to you anyway.

How Often

Don't just say that you play tennis — say how often you play tennis.

Learn these four adverbs

souvent: often
rarement: rarely
toujours: always
jamais: never

Il va rarement *en vacances.*

= He rarely goes on holiday.

Elle joue souvent *au tennis.*

= She often plays tennis.

These words don't change

Unlike normal describing words, the adverbs above
<u>don't change</u> for feminine, masculine or plural.

FOR EXAMPLE:

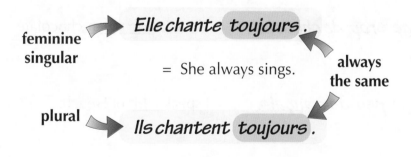

**feminine
singular** → *Elle chante* toujours *.*

= She always sings.

**always
the same**

plural → *Ils chantent* toujours *.*

= They always sing.

I study French always / often / rarely / never
Watch out if you want to say something like 'I go to Leeds a lot'. You actually mean 'I often go
to Leeds', so you should use <u>souvent</u> — 'Je vais souvent à Leeds'. Don't use 'beaucoup' here.

How Much

Here's another way to make your French sentences sound exciting — instead of saying 'Bob is happy', say Bob is 'quite happy' or 'very happy'.

A lot / a little — saying how much

Here's <u>very</u>, <u>quite</u>, <u>too</u> and <u>a bit</u> in French. You'll find that 'a bit' is really handy for answering questions in French about whether you speak French. Just say 'Oui, un peu' and you're sorted.

très *very*	*assez* *quite*
trop *too / too much*	*un peu* *a bit / a little*

Some examples of these words in action

Mon frère est très *fatigué.*   = My brother is <u>very</u> tired.

Elle mange trop *de chocolat.*   = She eats <u>too much</u> chocolate.

Je parle un peu *de français.*   = I speak <u>a bit</u> of French.

La chimie est assez *amusante.*   = Chemistry is <u>quite</u> fun.

---

*This is **very** boring, so now I'm **quite** tired*

This is another way to make your French sound more impressive. Instead of saying 'my brother is tall', say 'my brother is quite tall'. Just as uninteresting, but it might get you an extra mark.

Practice Questions

1 Copy out these sentences and write in the correct version of the verb 'vouloir', choosing from the ones in brackets.

a) Je .... (veux / veut) manger une glace.

b) Nous .... (veulent / voulons) aller à la piscine.

c) Il .... (veux / veut) acheter un vélo.

d) Elles .... (voulez / veulent) voir la vidéo.

e) Tu .... (veux / voulez) être médecin.

2 Copy out these sentences and add **à / à la / au** (to), **de** (of / from) or **pour** (for).

a) Je veux un litre .... lait. = I want a litre of milk.

b) Je vais .... collège. = I'm going to school.

c) Elle vient .... Calais. = She comes from Calais.

d) Nous voulons une tasse .... thé. = We want a cup of tea.

e) Il achète un livre .... son amie. = He buys a book for his friend.

3 Read this description of Philippe's bedroom, then write down whether the sentences below are true or false.

Ma chambre est assez grande. Mon lit est entre la porte et la fenêtre. Il y a une table à côté du lit, et sur la table il y a un ordinateur. Mon chien dort sous la table, et le chat dort sur le lit. En face du lit il y a une chaise, et devant la fenêtre il y a beaucoup de livres et de cassettes.

a) The door is next to the window.

b) The table is at the end of the bed.

c) The dog sleeps under the bed.

d) The chair is opposite the bed.

e) There are lots of books under the bed.

Practice Questions

4 Rewrite each pair of phrases by adding **et**. The first one has been done for you.

a) Je bois du lait. Je bois de la limonade.

Je bois du lait et de la limonade.

b) Marie va au marché. Marie va à la boulangerie.

c) Tu lis des livres. Tu lis des journaux.

5 Copy out the sentences below, and write either **mais** (but) or **parce que** (because) in the spaces, so that they make sense.

a) Je n'aime pas les oranges .... j'adore les bananes.

b) Je voudrais aller au cinéma, ... je dois finir mes devoirs.

c) Je voudrais aller au musée, ... c'est intéressant.

d) Je mange du chocolat .... j'aime beaucoup le chocolat.

e) Je parle français .... je ne parle pas japonais.

6 Write out the sentences below in French.

a) I always drink cold tea.

b) I never go to the beach.

c) I often go to Australia.

d) I rarely play golf.

7 Rewrite these sentences to show how much or how little people do things. The first one has been done for you.

a) Robert est fatigué. *(a little)* ....*Robert est un peu fatigué.*........................

b) Nous sommes contents. *(very)* ....

c) J'ai de l'eau. *(enough)* ....

d) Je travaille. *(too much)* ....

e) Il veut de la viande. *(a bit)* ....

Summary Questions

Bet you've been looking forward to this page, eh... Right. Brace yourselves. This is the Summary to end all Summaries. And to end the book. Now if that isn't incentive enough for you I don't know what is... You know the drill. Work your way through all these.

1) What do these mean in English?
a) J'aime le français parce que c'est utile.   b) J'adore le français.
c) Je déteste le français parce que c'est difficile.

2) What's the French word for each of these?
a) when?   b) where?   c) how much?   d) who?   e) which?

3) For each word, write down whether it's masculine or feminine and write down the plural:
a) le stylo   b) le gant   c) la pomme   d) le chocolat   e) la pharmacie

4) What are the French words for 'I', 'you' (informal, singular), 'he', 'she', 'we', 'you' (formal) and 'they'?

5) The French for 'the small man' is 'le petit homme'. What is the French for these?
a) the small men   b) the small girl   c) the small girls

6) The French for 'I am young' is 'Je suis jeune'. What do these mean in English?
a) Je suis plus jeune que Bob.   b) Je suis moins jeune que Bob.
c) Je suis aussi jeune que Bob.   d) Je suis le plus jeune.

7) 'Le chien' (dog) is masculine, and 'la tortue' (tortoise) is feminine.
How would you say these in French? I've done the first one for you.
a) my dog = mon chien   b) your (informal, singular) dog
c) your (formal) tortoises   d) our dogs   e) his tortoise   f) her tortoise
g) her dog   h) my dogs   i) this tortoise   j) this dog   k) these dogs

8) To say 'you' to these people, would you use 'tu' or 'vous'?
a) your younger sister   b) your older brother   c) a policeman   d) your teacher
e) your dad   f) a group of three friends   g) a group of three teachers

9) What do these mean in English?
a) je suis   b) ils ont   c) tu vas   d) nous sommes   e) nous allons

10) Write these out in French:
a) I'm not French.   b) I never go to France.   c) I don't eat anything.

11) These are in the present tense. Write them out in the future tense.
The infinitive is in brackets.
a) Je regarde la télé. (regarder)   b) Elle parle à Jacques. (parler)
c) Vous mangez. (manger)

12) What do these mean in English?
a) J'ai mangé une banane.   b) Vous avez joué au tennis.

13) What do these mean?   a) Je veux manger.   b) Vous pouvez jouer.

14) What are the French words for 'and' and 'or'?

15) Write down the French for 'I like cats but I don't like dogs'.
('J'aime les chats.' = I like cats. 'Je n'aime pas les chiens.' = I don't like dogs.)

Page 6

1 a) deux + trois = cinq
   b) quatre + sept = onze
   c) un + douze = treize
   d) neuf + huit = dix-sept
   e) vingt - deux = dix-huit

2 a) 3   b) 5   c) 4   d) 2   e) 1   f) 6

3 a) le trois août   b) le dix avril
   c) le vingt-cinq décembre   d) le quatorze mars
   e) le dix-huit février   f) le trente-et-un octobre
   g) le premier juillet   h) le vingt-sept janvier

Pages 14-15

1 a) salut   b) bonne nuit   c) au revoir
   d) bonjour   e) à bientôt

2 a) Salut, Gérard, ça va?   b) Bonsoir, enchanté(e).
   c) Je vous/te présente mon ami(e). d) À bientôt/à plus tard.
   e) Il s'appelle Robert.   f) Bonne nuit, mes ami(e)s.
   g) Je vous/te présente Henri.

3 a) F   b) T   c) F   d) T   e) F

4 Merci   quelle heure est-il?
   Je voudrais   je n'aime pas les fraises.
   Excusez-moi, mais   s'il vous plaît.
   Deux cafés   beaucoup.
   Pardon, monsieur,   du beurre.

5 a) 2   b) 1   c) 4   d) 3

6 a) Est-ce que je peux aller au cinéma?
   b) Est-ce que je peux faire la vaisselle?
   c) Est-ce que je peux faire la cuisine?
   d) Est-ce que je peux mettre la table?

Pages 25-26

1 a) I am sporty. I like football.
   b) I am shy but nice.
   c) I am lazy. I like music.
   d) I am hard-working. I like school.

2 a) Je m'appelle [your name].
   b) J'ai [your age] ans.
   c) Mon anniversaire est le [day, month].

3 a) Je m'appelle Daphne. Je suis grande. J'ai les yeux verts. J'ai les cheveux roux/Je suis rousse.
   b) Je m'appelle Velma. Je suis petite. Je suis grosse. J'ai les yeux marron. Je porte des lunettes.
   c) Je m'appelle Fred. Je suis de taille moyenne. Je suis mince. J'ai les yeux bleus. J'ai les cheveux blonds/Je suis blond.
   d) Je m'appelle M. Shaggy. Je suis grand. J'ai les cheveux assez longs. J'ai les yeux verts.

4 a) Michel (step-father)
   b) Chantal (step-mother)
   c) Emilie (sister)
   d) Jean-Luc (brother)
   e) Julien (half-brother)
   f) Marie (half-sister)

5 a) J'ai un chien. Mon chien s'appelle Fang. Il est grand, noir et méchant.
   b) J'ai une tortue. Ma tortue s'appelle Fred. Ma tortue est petite et verte.
   c) J'ai un hamster. Mon hamster s'appelle Bubbles. Mon hamster est petit et mignon.
   d) J'ai un oiseau. Mon oiseau s'appelle Nipper. Mon oiseau est très méchant.

6 a) Tom.
   b) It's big and nasty.
   c) He has a mouse. It's sweet.
   d) He doesn't have a pet.

7 a) kitchen, living room, two bedrooms
   b) Sophie
   c) Sophie
   d) Paul
   e) bed, chair(s)

Pages 35-36

1 a) In a flat.
   b) In a house.
   c) In a village.
   d) In a town.
   e) In a big town/city.

2 a) T   b) T   c) F   d) F   e) T

3 Je me réveille à sept heures — I wake up at seven o'clock.
   Je me lave à sept heures et demie — I get washed at half past seven.
   Je mange le petit déjeuner à huit heures — I eat breakfast at eight o'clock.
   Je vais à l'école à huit heures et demie. — I go to school at half past eight.
   Je rentre à la maison à seize heures. — I return home at four o'clock.
   À dix-sept heures je regarde la télé. — At five o'clock I watch the telly.
   Je prends le dîner à vingt heures. — I have dinner at eight o'clock.
   Je me couche à vingt-deux heures. — I go to bed at ten o'clock.

4 a) Kate: Je lave la voiture et je passe l'aspirateur.
   b) Brian: Je fais la vaisselle et je fais les courses.
   c) Kavita: Je range ma chambre et je fais mon lit.
   d) Richard: Je mets la table et je fais le ménage.
   e) Thomas: Je ne fais rien.

5 A la tête   B l'estomac   C le bras   D la main
   E le doigt   F le cou   G le dos   H la jambe
   I le genou   J le pied

6 a) au   b) aux   c) à la
   d) à la   e) à la   f) à l'

7 a) He has stomach ache.
   b) He wants to go to the doctor's.
   c) Marie
   d) Marie
   e) She wants to go to the hospital.

Pages 47-48

1 a) T b) F c) T d) F e) T

2 a) Je me lève à sept heures.
   b) Je vais au collège/à l'école en vélo.
   c) Les cours commencent à huit heures et demie.
   d) Je fais une heure de devoirs par jour.

3 Il y a 30 élèves dans ma classe. Le professeur s'appelle John Smith. J'écris les exercices dans mon cahier avec un crayon. Quand je fais une erreur je l'efface avec la gomme. L'anglais, c'est cool.

4 a) maçon   b) dentiste   c) gendarme
   d) professeur   e) médecin   f) secrétaire

5 a) On foot.
   b) She is a secretary.
   c) No — he's a salesperson.
   d) He works in Monsieur Bricolage.
   e) His father.
   f) A part-time job (as a hairdresser).
   g) He wants to be an engineer.

Page 55

1 a) T   b) F   c) T   d) T
2 a) la piscine
  b) le cinéma
  c) la poste
  d) la banque
  e) le syndicat d'initiative / l'office de tourisme
  f) la gare
3 a) la boulangerie   b) la pâtisserie   c) la librairie
  d) la pharmacie   e) la boucherie   f) la charcuterie

Pages 64-65

1 Fruit: la fraise, la poire, la pêche, la pomme
  Veg: le champignon, le chou-fleur, l'oignon, la carotte
  Meat: le porc, le saucisson, le poulet, la saucisse
2 a) la crème   b) le beurre   c) le yaourt
  d) l'oeuf   e) le biscuit   f) la confiture
  g) le sucre   h) le chocolat   i) le gâteau
  j) le fromage
3 crisps, biscuits, sugar, ham, cheese, a lemon.
4 a) J'aime les bananes.   b) Je n'aime pas le café.
  c) Je suis végétarien(ne).   d) Je n'aime pas la crème.
5 a) 7.30am
  b) chicken and salad
  c) lunch
6 a) Je voudrais réserver une table pour quatre personnes, s'il vous plaît.
  b) Vous désirez?
  c) Avez-vous du steak?
  d) Je voudrais de l'eau minérale.
  e) Je voudrais l'addition, s'il vous plaît.

Page 70

1 a) Je porte une robe rouge.
  b) Pierre porte un manteau en cuir.
  c) Elle porte un chemisier vert.
  d) Il porte un imperméable gris.
  e) Thierry porte un pull en laine.
  f) Tu portes/vous portez un tee-shirt rose.
  g) Nous portons des manteaux noirs.
2 a) un euro soixante-dix
  b) deux euros trente-cinq
  c) cinq euros quatre-vingt-cinq
  d) dix euros douze
3 a) I'll take it.
  b) Is that all?
  c) How much is it?
4 a) blue
  b) a (green) blouse
  c) 30,25 euros

Page 78

1 a) de la   b) de la   c) du   d) de la
  e) au   f) aux   g) de la   h) du
2 a) Je fais du ski parce que c'est amusant.
  b) Je fais les courses parce que c'est facile.
  c) Je n'aime pas le football parce que c'est difficile.
  d) J'aime le cyclisme parce que c'est intéressant.
  e) Je déteste la natation parce que c'est ennuyeux.

3 a) Oui, j'aime ce film.
  b) Non, je n'aime pas ce film.
  c) Oui, j'aime ce roman.
  d) Non, je n'aime pas ce magazine.
  e) Non, je n'aime pas ce journal.
  f) Oui, j'aime cette musique.
  g) Oui, j'aime ce livre.
4 a) Albert   b) Francine   c) Serge   d) Francine
  e) Serge   f) Juliette   g) Juliette   h) Albert

Pages 86-87

1 a) au centre-ville   b) à la piscine   c) au restaurant
  d) chez moi   e) au cinéma   f) chez toi
2 a) Non merci, je n'ai pas d'argent.
  b) Oui, je veux bien.
  c) Non, je fais mes devoirs.
  d) Non merci, je n'aime pas le centre de loisirs.
  e) Oui, bonne idée — j'adore le cinéma.
3 a) Let's meet tomorrow, at the swimming pool.
  b) Let's meet this morning, in the town centre.
  c) Let's meet on Monday, at my place.
  d) Let's meet at the restaurant at eight o'clock.
4 a) On se retrouve où?
  b) Combien coûte un billet?
  c) Je voudrais deux billets, s'il vous plaît.
  d) On se retrouve quand ?
  e) Un billet coûte trois euros.
5 a) en bateau   b) en (auto)bus / car   c) à pied
  d) en moto   e) en voiture   f) en vélo
6 a) Je voudrais un aller simple pour Toulouse, en deuxième classe.
  b) Je voudrais un aller-retour pour Paris, en deuxième classe.
  c) Je voudrais un aller simple pour Nice, en première classe.
  d) Je voudrais un aller simple pour Calais, en deuxième classe.
  e) Je voudrais un aller-retour pour Marseille, en première classe.

7

Destination	Heure	Quai
Bordeaux	7.20	6
Dijon	8.45	3
Le Mans	11.30	1
Nantes	14.15	4
Perpignan	16.25	2
Rouen	18.05	5

Page 93

1 a) I would like a three-euro stamp.
  b) How much is it ?
  c) I would like to send a letter to France.
  d) I'd like two four-euro stamps.
2 a) Allô — **ici** Magalie.
  b) Mon **numéro** de **téléphone** est le dix-sept, cinquante, vingt-deux.
  c) Je **peux parler** à James?
3 The letter can vary, but here's one you could write:
    Kendal, le 2 mai
    Chère Marie,
    Comment ça va? Merci de ta lettre.
    Je suis très content(e) de recevoir
    de tes nouvelles. Écris-moi vite!
    À bientôt,
    Bunty
4 a) a hotel
  b) single
  c) 5 nights

d) January

e) how much it is

Pages 103-104

1 a) In winter.

b) Because it snows.

c) It's bad weather, it's cloudy and it rains a lot.

d) Spring and autumn.

e) It's sunny and hot.

2 a) il pleut

b) il fait chaud

c) il neige

d) il y a de l'orage (*or* il tonne, *or* il y a des éclairs)

e) il est ensoleillé/ il fait (du) soleil

f) il fait du vent/il y a du vent/il vente.

3 a) Spain

b) his Dad, his Mum and the dog

c) ten days

d) in a hotel

e) he watches television

f) when it's sunny

4 Answers could vary for these. Here's what you could write:

a) Je vais en Italie avec ma mère pour trois semaines.

b) Je vais en Allemagne pour une semaine. Je reste dans un camping.

c) Je vais en France et je vais à la plage.

d) Je vais en Écosse. Il fait (du) soleil.

5 a) youth hostel

b) telephone

c) dining room

d) hotel

e) toilets

f) key

g) bathroom

h) campsite

6 a) Une chambre individuelle / pour une personne avec douche.

b) Une chambre double / pour deux personnes avec bain / salle de bains.

c) Une chambre individuelle / pour une personne avec balcon.

d) Une chambre double / pour deux personnes avec douche et balcon.

7 a) T   b) F   c) T   d) T   e) F

8 Avez-vous des emplacements libres?

Je voudrais un emplacement pour une tente, s'il vous plaît.

Je voudrais rester quatre nuits. C'est combien?

Page 109

1 a) l'Angleterre   b) le Pays de Galles

c) l'Écosse   d) l'Irlande du Nord

2 a) The Netherlands   b) Germany   c) Belgium

d) France   e) UK   f) Austria

g) Switzerland   h) Italy   i) Spain

j) Portugal   k) Great Britain

3 b) Je suis écossaise.   c) Je suis gallois.   d) Je suis anglais.

4 a) France   b) Manuel and Maria   c) Italy

d) German   e) Irish   f) England

g) Wales

Page 117

1 a) Je n'aime pas le football parce que c'est ennuyeux.

b) J'aime la chimie parce que c'est utile.

c) J'adore regarder la télévision parce que c'est intéressant.

d) Je déteste le collège parce que c'est difficile.

2 a) How old are you?

b) How much does this book cost?

c) Where do you live?

d) When's your birthday?

e) Who is this girl?

f) Where is the theatre?

3 a) J'ai deux chats.

b) Il aime deux filles.

c) Pierre mange deux gâteaux.

d) Claire a deux frères.

e) Il a deux animaux.

Page 124

1 a) Je vais à l'école. I go to school.

b) Je vais à la piscine. I go to the swimming pool.

c) Je joue au football. I play football.

d) Ils jouent aux échecs. They play chess.

e) Nous allons au cinéma. We go to the cinema.

2 a) une règle   b) un cahier   c) une classe

d) une pomme   e) un lapin   f) une télévision

g) un garçon   h) une chambre   i) un sac

3 a) Je le mange.   b) Jean les aime.   c) Elle la regarde.

d) Vous les lavez.   e) Ils le lisent.   f) Tu le bois.

Pages 133-134

1 a) J'ai une grande maison.

b) Il a des yeux verts.

c) Elles sont petites.

d) Ton père est gentil.

e) Dans mon collège il y a beaucoup de belles filles.

f) Ma grand-mère est une vieille femme.

2 a) Tom est grand, mais Mark est plus grand.

b) Sophie est belle, mais Marie est plus belle.

c) Suresh est mince, mais Frank est plus mince.

d) Ton père est gentil, mais mon père est plus gentil.

3 a) Le livre est meilleur que le film.

b) Le français est pire que l'allemand.

c) Je danse mieux que toi.

d) Mon père est meilleur que ton père.

4 a) Mon frère a 15 ans.

b) Sa voiture est rouge.

c) Ton/votre chien est méchant.

d) J'ai mangé son sandwich.

e) Il y a 200 élèves dans mon collège.

f) Sa soeur déteste ton frère.

g) Où sont tes chaussettes?

5 a) cette souris

b) ces chaussures

c) ce stylo

d) cet enfant

e) cette glace

f) ce fromage

g) cette orange

h) ces chiens

i) cet hôpital

6 a) Est-ce que tu as faim?

b) Est-ce que vous parlez anglais?

c) Comment tu t'appelles?

d) Je déteste vos cours.

e) J'aime tes chaussures.

Pages 141-142

1 a) je comprends   b) tu perds

c) il prend   d) nous descendons

e) vous attendez   f) ils/elles mordent

2 a) sommes   b) allons

c) ont   d) êtes

e) avons   f) allez

g) sont   h) avez

3 a) 16   b) Luc

c) 9   d) Francine

e) mother   f) dog

4 a) Je suis anglais(e).   b) J'ai treize ans.

c) J'ai un chien.   d) Claude a une soeur.

5 a) c'est   b) il y a

c) il y a   d) c'est

6 a) Bobo se réveille.   b) Bobo se lève.

c) Bobo se brosse les dents.   d) Bobo s'habille.

e) Bobo se couche.

7 a) se   b) nous

c) me   d) vous

e) se   f) te

g) m'

Pages 151-152

1 a) F   b) F

c) T   d) F

e) T   f) T

2 a) Je **ne** me lève **pas** à six heures.

b) Je **ne** suis **pas** français.

c) Tu **ne** manges **rien** à midi.

d) Nous **ne** parlons **jamais** en classe.

3 a) Nous allons   b) Il va

c) Ils vont   d) Je vais

e) Tu vas

4 a) come in   b) walk

c) don't smoke   d) pull

e) don't touch   f) push

5 a) marche   b) mange

c) joue   d) tombe

6 À neuf heures j'ai téléphoné à mon ami Henri, et nous avons décidé d'aller au centre-ville. J'ai marché au centre à pied, mais mon ami a choisi l'autobus. Nous avons regardé les boutiques et nous avons acheté un CD et des glaces. Après, nous avons joué au tennis de table.

7 a) J'ai mangé une banane.

b) J'ai commencé les cours.

c) J'ai parlé avec mes amis.

d) J'ai déjeuné.

e) J'ai joué au tennis.

Pages 161-162

1 a) veux

b) voulons

c) veut

d) veulent

e) veux

2 a) de

b) au

c) de

d) de

e) pour

3 a) F

b) F

c) F

d) T

e) F

4 a) Je bois du lait et de la limonade.

b) Marie va au marché et à la boulangerie.

c) Tu lis des livres et des journaux.

5 a) mais

b) mais

c) parce que

d) parce que

e) mais

6 a) Je bois toujours du thé froid.

b) Je ne vais jamais à la plage.

c) Je vais souvent en Australie.

d) Je joue rarement au golf.

7 a) Robert est un peu fatigué.

b) Nous sommes très contents.

c) J'ai assez d'eau.

d) Je travaille trop.

e) Il veut un peu de viande.

Section 1

Track 1, Page 6
Question 2
a)

F1   Il est une heure et demie.

b)

M1   Il est cinq heures et quart.

c)

F2   Il est deux heures vingt-cinq.

d)

M2   Il est quatre heures et quart.

e)

F1   Il est trois heures cinq.

f)

M1   Il est sept heures moins vingt.

Track 2, Page 14
Question 3
a)

M1   Bonsoir, Sophie. Comment vas-tu?

F1   Bonsoir, Monsieur Dupont. Ça va bien, merci.

b)

F2   À bientôt, Marc.

M2   À plus tard, Emilie.

c)

F1   Je vous présente Madame Ferret.

M1   Enchanté.

d)

M2   Salut, Gaëlle. Ça va?

F2   Salut, Robert. Ça va bien, merci.

e)

M1   Au revoir, Madame Marnier.

F1   Au revoir, Monsieur le Président.

Track 3, Page 15
Question 5
a)

F1   Excusez-moi, mais j'ai oublié votre nom.

b)

M1   Excusez-moi, mais je n'ai pas de fromage.

c)

F2   Excusez-moi, mais je suis végétarienne.

d)

M2   Excusez-moi, mais je n'aime pas la natation.

Section 2

Track 4, Page 25
Question 4

M1   J'ai une grande famille! J'habite avec ma mère, qui s'appelle Monique, et mon beau-père, qui s'appelle Michel. Mon père s'appelle Charles. Il habite avec ma belle-mère, qui s'appelle Chantal. J'ai un frère et une sœur. Mon frère s'appelle Jean-Luc et ma sœur s'appelle Emilie. J'ai aussi une demi-sœur, qui s'appelle Marie, et un demi-frère, qui s'appelle Julien. Marie et Julien habitent avec mon père et ma belle-mère.

Track 5, Page 26
Question 7

M1   Qu'est-ce qu'il y a chez toi, Pierre?

M2   Chez moi, il y a quatre pièces. Il y a une cuisine, un salon et deux chambres.

M1   Très bien. Qu'est-ce qu'il y a chez toi, Sophie?

F1   Chez moi, il y a six pièces. Il y a trois chambres, une salle à manger, une salle de bains et une cuisine.

M1   C'est une très grande maison, alors! Qu'est-ce qu'il y a dans ta chambre?

F1   Il y a un lit, une armoire, un canapé et deux chaises.

M1   Et qu'est-ce qu'il y a dans ta chambre, Pierre?

M2   Dans ma chambre, il y a un lit, un placard, une table et une chaise.

Track 6, Page 35
Question 2

M1   Je m'appelle François. J'habite à Paris, une grande ville dans le nord de la France. J'aime habiter ici parce que c'est intéressant.

F1   Je m'appelle Marie. J'habite à Bourg St. Andéol, un village dans le sud de la France. Je n'aime pas habiter ici parce que c'est trop tranquille.

M2   Je m'appelle Marc. J'habite à Bordeaux, une ville dans le sud-ouest de la France. J'aime habiter ici parce que c'est tranquille.

F2   Je m'appelle Chantal. J'habite à Strasbourg, une ville dans le nord-est de la France. Je n'aime pas habiter ici parce que c'est ennuyeux.

Track 7, Page 36
Question 7

M1   Je suis malade. J'ai mal au ventre. Je veux aller chez le médecin pour une ordonnance.

F1   Je suis malade aussi. Moi, j'ai mal à la tête, j'ai mal aux dents et j'ai mal à la gorge. Je veux aller à l'hôpital.

Section 3

Track 8, Page 47
Question 1

M1   À l'école, j'étudie beaucoup de matières. J'étudie les sciences, l'histoire, le dessin, les maths, le français, l'anglais… enfin beaucoup. J'aime l'anglais et les maths. Je déteste le français. Ma matière préférée est le dessin.

Section 4

Track 9, Page 55
Question 1
a)

M1   Excusez-moi, pour aller à la banque, s'il vous plaît?

F1   Eh bien, vous allez tout droit, et la banque est sur votre gauche.

M1   Merci bien, Madame.

b)

F2   Pardon, Monsieur, où est le supermarché, s'il vous plaît?

M2   Tournez à droite, et le supermarché est en face.

F2   Merci, au revoir.

c)

F1   Excusez-moi, Madame, pour aller à la gare, s'il vous plaît?

F2   Prenez la deuxième rue à droite.

F1   Merci.

d)

F2   Excusez-moi, Monsieur, où est la boucherie, s'il vous plaît?

M1   Allez tout droit.

F2   C'est loin d'ici?

M1   Assez loin; c'est à deux kilomètres d'ici.

F2   Merci bien. Au revoir.

Track 10, Page 64
Question 3

F1   Je voudrais beaucoup de choses. Alors, je voudrais un paquet de chips, trois paquets de biscuits et deux paquets de sucre. Puis, de la charcuterie, je voudrais quatre tranches de jambon. Je voudrais aussi 200g de fromage, mais je ne veux pas de lait. Je n'aime pas le lait! Tu peux m'acheter un citron, aussi? Merci, c'est gentil.

Track 11, Page 65
Question 5

F2   Je prends mon petit déjeuner à sept heures et demie. D'habitude, je mange du pain et je bois du café. Le déjeuner est à midi. On mange un sandwich au jambon ou un sandwich au fromage. Le soir, je dîne à dix-neuf heures. Je mange du poulet et de la salade, et je bois un jus d'orange.

Track 12, Page 70
Question 4

F1   Bonjour, Madame. Je peux vous aider?

F2   Oui, avez-vous une jupe bleue?

F1   Oui, voilà.

F2   Merci, je l'aime bien, je la prends.

F1   C'est tout?

F2   Non, je voudrais aussi un chemisier vert.

F1   Voilà. Ça fait trente euros vingt-cinq.

F2   Merci bien. Au revoir.

F1   De rien. Au revoir.

Section 5

Track 13, Page 78
Question 4

M1   Je m'appelle Serge. J'aime écouter de la musique, mais je n'aime pas regarder de films.

F1   Je m'appelle Francine. J'écoute la radio, mais je ne lis pas de romans.

M2   Je m'appelle Albert. Je lis des livres, mais je n'aime pas regarder la télévision.

F2   Je m'appelle Juliette. Je n'aime pas lire les journaux, mais je regarde des films.

Track 14, Page 87
Question 7
a)

M1   Le train pour Dijon part de quel quai?

F1   Du quai numéro 3, Monsieur.

b)

M2   Le train pour Rouen part de quel quai?

F1   Le train part du quai numéro 5.

c)

F2   À quelle heure part le train pour Nantes?

M1   Alors... à 14h15.

d)

F2   À quelle heure part le train pour Perpignan?

M2   Le train part à 16h25.

Section 7

Track 15, Page 103
Question 1

F1   Au printemps, il fait beau mais il pleut souvent. En hiver, il fait froid, mais l'hiver est ma saison préférée parce qu'il neige. En automne, il fait mauvais, il y a des nuages et il pleut beaucoup. En été, il y a du soleil et il fait chaud.

Track 16, Page 104
Question 7

M1   Bonjour, Madame.

F1   Bonjour, est-ce que je peux vous aider?

M1   Avez-vous des chambres de libre?

F1   Oui Monsieur, que voulez-vous comme chambres?

M1   Nous voudrions une chambre double, avec salle de bains, et une chambre individuelle pour notre fille.

F1   C'est pour combien de nuits?

M1   Nous voudrions rester cinq nuits. C'est combien?

F1   Alors, une chambre double coûte 100 euros la nuit, et une chambre individuelle coûte 60 euros la nuit, donc cela fait 800 euros pour cinq nuits. Le petit déjeuner est compris.

M1   Merci beaucoup.

Track 17, Page 109
Question 4

M1   Je suis français. J'habite en France.

Francesca est italienne — elle habite en Italie.

Gerhard est allemand, et Manuel est espagnol.

Peter est anglais et Maria est espagnole.

Gerry est irlandais, mais il habite en Angleterre.

Lisa est galloise.

Section 8

Track 18, Page 141
Question 3

M2   Je m'appelle Claude. Je suis français et j'ai seize ans. J'ai un frère et une sœur. Mon frère s'appelle Luc, il a neuf ans, et il va à l'école. Ma sœur s'appelle Francine, elle a quatorze ans et elle va au collège. Chez nous, il y a aussi mes parents, bien sûr. Ils s'appellent Jean et Marie. Nous avons aussi un chien. Il est très grand, mais très mignon.

Track 19, Page 151
Question 1

F1   Jean-Pierre est français, de Paris. Il a seize ans. Il aime la natation et la musique. Il a un chat, mais il habite dans un appartement, alors il n'a pas de chien. Il mange beaucoup de bananes mais il n'aime pas les oranges. Sa sœur s'appelle Monique et son frère s'appelle Maurice.

Transcript of the Audio CD

Index

Index

Make sure you're not missing out on another superb CGP revision book that might just save your life...

...order your **free** catalogue today.

CGP customer service is second to none

We work very hard to despatch all orders the **same day** we receive them, and our success rate is currently 99.9%. We send all orders by **overnight courier** or **First Class** post.
If you ring us today you should get your catalogue or book tomorrow. Irresistible, surely?

- Phone: 0870 750 1252   (Mon-Fri, 8.30am to 5.30pm)
- Fax: 0870 750 1292
- e-mail: orders@cgpbooks.co.uk
- Post: CGP Orders, Broughton-in-Furness, Cumbria, LA20 6BN
- Website: www.cgpbooks.co.uk

...or you can ask at any good bookshop.